Creating Suspense
in
Fiction

Creating Suspense in Fiction

JOHN PAXTON SHERIFF

ROBERT HALE · LONDON

© *John Paxton Sheriff 1999*
First published in Great Britain 1999

ISBN 0 7090 6428 4

Robert Hale Limited
Clerkenwell House
Clerkenwell Green
London EC1R 0HT

2 4 6 8 10 9 7 5 3 1

Typeset in 10/15 Palatino by
Derek Doyle & Associates, Mold, Flintshire.
Printed in Great Britain by
St Edmundsbury Press Limited, Bury St Edmunds,
and bound by
WBC Book Manufacturers Ltd, Bridgend.

Contents

Acknowledgements

For permission to use extracts from various novels in this book, my thanks go to the following:

Curtis Brown Ltd on behalf of the Estate of Ralph Hammond Innes for *The Mary Deare* by Hammond Innes.

Peters, Fraser & Dunlop Group Ltd for *In Honour Bound* by Gerald Seymour.

HarperCollins Publishers Ltd for *The Ghosts of Sleath* by James Herbert; *Morning Glory* by LaVyrle Spencer; *Nothing Lasts Forever* and *If Tomorrow Comes* by Sidney Sheldon.

Orion Publishing Group Ltd for *A Stab in the Dark* by Lawrence Block.

A.M. Heath & Co. Ltd for *A Stranger Is Watching* by Mary Higgins Clark; *The Scorpion Signal* by Adam Hall.

Random House, Inc. for *The Runaway Jury* by John Grisham; *Our Game* by John le Carré.

Transworld Publishers Ltd for *Malice* by Danielle Steel.

Hodder and Stoughton Limited for *Christine, The Tommyknockers* and *Insomnia* by Stephen King; *Tinker, Tailor, Soldier, Spy* by John le Carré; *Timothy's Game* by Lawrence Sanders; *Gladly the Cross-Eyed Bear* by Ed McBain.

Little, Brown & Co. UK for *From Potter's Field* by Patricia Daniels Cornwell.

Penguin Books Ltd for *Straight* by Dick Francis; *Banker* by Dick Francis; *The Big Sleep* by Raymond Chandler.

Introduction

The two words suspense and tension are inextricably linked.

One dictionary definition of suspense is a state of anxious uncertainty or expectation, while tension can be defined as mental strain or excitement. They say that we are in one, and feel the other.

Whether one causes the other – and which is the cause and which the effect – is a moot point, though logic tells us that an increase in suspense will create in us all a feeling of tension; we worry, and so we become highly strung. But what is inarguable is that no work of fiction will succeed if it does not induce in the reader both those conditions.

Of course, suspense and tension are there already, in all of us. We go through life always wondering what will happen next, whether we will succeed or fail; and the seriousness of the situation will determine the amount of suspense we are in and the tension we feel (they call it stress, nowadays, and we are under it, not feeling it). It is quite possible that some people become listless and bored and eventually fade away when they retire, simply because the excitement has gone out of their lives. Suspense and tension are not there in sufficient quantities to make life interesting, so they close the book.

In life and in books, the excitement (caused by those now familiar conditions) comes in different degrees, and in different forms, though the form does not necessarily determine the degree. The businessman chewing his nails over the outcome of a million-dollar merger will be suffering a different kind of suspense from that experienced by a condemned man on his way to the electric chair with one ear cocked for the telephone call that will grant him a reprieve – but each, in his own way, will be considering the result a matter of life and death.

This apparent paradox is helpful to authors, because it means that tension can be created in books as diverse as a children's adventure by Roald Dahl or an adult thriller by Adam Hall simply by the application of the form of suspense suited to the genre.

This book will take the mystery out of creating suspense mainly by hammering home the lesson that there is no suspense without mystery. People worry about what is going to happen in life; people reading books worry about what is going to happen to other people (although, as you will see, knowing exactly what is going to happen before it actually happens can make the suspense unbearable.)

As well as talking through my own ideas and theories, I have used extracts from books by many bestselling authors to illustrate suspense techniques as familiar as cliffhangers and as obscure as foreshadowing and linked scenes within chapters.

If I have done my job, you will know yours better, and through the blatant exploitation of suspense I will have achieved what must always be the aim and written a book that you, the reader, simply cannot put down.

1 Creating Suspense with Atmospheric Scenes and Settings

This book is about the creation of suspense, and although much mention will be made of such divisions as scenes, chapters and parts, there will be no attempt to make you change the structure of your novel.

By the time you come to read this book you may already have decided that the book you are going to write will begin with a prologue, that there will then be parts one, two and three, each of which will be introduced by a quotation. The novel may already be written.

But those are simply labels for sections, and unless you have convinced readers at the beginning – either in that prologue, or at the start of a riveting first chapter – that the novel that follows is going to be worth reading, then the first section they read may well be the last.

However, before you begin the job of convincing readers – and start using the techniques described from Chapter Four onwards to ensure that they keep reading to the very last page – you must make sure that in your opening you are not very cleverly deceiving them into believing something that simply isn't true. In other words, you must do your best to ensure that what you are about to write really will be interesting, even memorable.

To make it memorable you must build suspense into the very fabric of your novel, and your first step along this path is to think hard about the picture you are going to paint on that fabric.

So, why atmospheric scenes and settings?

We live in a visual age. People tell us this as if it were something new, when of course it has always been so. People used their eyes to see long before they picked up a quill to write; one picture is still better than a thousand words. Nothing is so instantly evocative, and because of films, television, other books or even, occasionally, actual experience, people have been conditioned to anticipate a particular theme for each given location.

It's a kind of image stereotyping; the equivalent of the use of white hats and black hats to denote 'goodies' and 'baddies' in Westerns.

This chapter will show you how to:

- Use rugged scenery to suggest high adventure
- Create a Gothic atmosphere to suggest horror
- Place characters in inner-city landscapes to suggest violence
- Use a big-business environment to suggest intrigue
- Make a fashion/media scene suggest sexual tension

Use Rugged Scenery to Suggest High Adventure

The structure of an adventure novel is usually much less complicated than that of a thriller. Most are linear, or chronological; they start at point A and make directly for point Z at a truly hectic pace. Flash-backs are kept to a minimum, and heroes and heroines play out the drama against a rugged backdrop that can range from an exotic location in the tropics to an Antarctic landscape swept by blizzards.

I was tired, and cold. A little scared, too. The red and green navigation lights cast a weird glow over the sails. Beyond was nothing, a void of utter darkness in which the sea made little rushing noises. I eased my legs, sucking on a piece of barley sugar. Above me the sails swung in a ghostly arc, slatting back and forth as *Sea Witch* rolled and plunged . . . God! It was cold! Cold and clammy – and not a star anywhere.

© Hammond Innes 1956. Extract from *The Mary Deare* by Hammond Innes. Reproduced with permission of Curtis Brown Ltd, London, on behalf of the Estate of Ralph Hammond Innes.

This is part of the long paragraph that Hammond Innes uses to carry his readers into the chill atmosphere of his no ￢l. The setting is brilliantly painted, both through vivid descriptive phrases and the reactions of the main character.

Although this chapter is always going to be more concerned with how we can establish an environment in which suspense of various kinds can flourish than with the actual *creation* of suspense, it is interesting to note that in the quoted paragraph the author, as well as painting a picture, has already begun to build suspense. Notice that the man in the boat is tired, and cold – and a little scared. The boat is named *'Sea Witch'*; its sails swing in a ghostly arc; there is not a star to be seen.

Readers will be aware that something is about to happen. At sea this will almost certainly be an encounter with another ship, and so it turns out. Not too long after the opening sequence the *Sea Witch* narrowly avoids a disastrous collision with the *Mary Deare*, and the reader becomes embroiled in the high conflict between the hero and the mysterious 'Patch'.

In *In Honour Bound*, Gerald Seymour takes us far away from the sea into the mountains of Afghanistan. In the opening paragraph he paints a picture and sets a scene that will, apart from some necessary, temporary departures, be the setting for the rest of the book. And do take note of that. It is absolutely imperative that, if you draw your readers into an adventure novel that promises an exotic setting, you do not cheat them by having the main action take place elsewhere. Occasionally you may stray elsewhere, as the action unfolds. But in almost all cases, the scene set at the beginning of a book will be the scene of the climax.

They had been coming back for four days.

Four, crippling, painful days of tramping out a stride cross the knife rock of the mountains. Brutal days because the pace was set by a guide who moved as if he were ignorant of the bitter sharp of the stone and the scree as they climbed, then descended, then climbed again. When they moved by day there was the ferocious heat of the sun. And when they travelled by night there were bruising falls and the stumbles and the cutting of the rock on their shins and knees and hands and elbows.

© Gerald Seymour 1984. Extract from *In Honour Bound* by Gerald Seymour. Reprinted by permission of Peters, Fraser & Dunlop Group Ltd.

Notice how the suspense is not stated, but subtly implied in the very first sentence. 'They had been coming back for four days.' Coming back from where?, the reader wonders with a chill of apprehension. Clearly they have not yet reached the place from which they set out, and for there to be so much urgency, danger must lie behind them. But what is the threat – and fleeing over such rugged terrain, just how much longer can they go on, or survive?

A hundred years ago a book with this setting would plant in readers' minds images of ferocious tribesmen with curved swords, of stalwart adventurers forever searching the narrow ravines for the flash of sun on metal, the flicker of a white robe.

In Gerald Seymour's book those same tribesmen are there, but are now armed with modern rifles. Move the location a few thousand miles in either direction and, while the scenery may be similar, the threat might come from Mexican bandits swooping from the high sierras, or from hard-eyed men employed by multi-national organizations searching for rich mineral deposits in dense jungle.

Create a Gothic Atmosphere to Suggest Horror

Horror novels are suspense in the raw. At their crudest – and this is not meant in a derogatory way – Gothic horror novels tell of sinister counts inhabiting dank castles, lightning hissing over barren moors, and cowering, terrified maidens listening for the beat of horses' hooves that will mean rescue is at hand.

Although Edgar Allan Poe was a poet and short story writer, the methods he used to create an atmosphere of horror that was almost pure suspense can be of great help to would-be Gothic novelists. Nowadays, many horror/supernatural novels have modern settings, yet because of the nature of the genre the setting can still adhere closely to those classic Gothic principles: dark buildings set in a brooding landscape; the dazzling flash of lightning over pitted gravestones and the rumble of distant thunder; water cascading darkly over a weir as the skeletal trees toss in the rising wind.

In 1994, James Herbert chose an excellent, evocative title – *The Ghosts of Sleath* – and used typical Gothic imagery in the opening pages:

Spiders weaved webs among the hedges of a lane and a carrion crow skimmed low along its dusty length. The bird abruptly soared above the treetops, then swooped down again to perch on a tilted gravestone in the cemetery beyond . . . An ancient church, its stonework scarred and worn by centuries of inclement weather but brightened this day by unhindered sunlight, rose high over the proceedings, and dark lancet windows within the tower's walls seemed to watch the assembly with the crow.

© James Herbert 1994. Extract from *The Ghosts of Sleath* by James Herbert. Reproduced by permission of HarperCollins Publishers Ltd.

This is a scene rich in possibilities for the author intent on building suspense within the bounds of the horror genre.

Although the book begins at a fairly leisurely pace, the sombre atmosphere created in the first few pages skilfully prepares readers to expect the worst. In the next few lines a child's coffin is mentioned, and a woman standing apart from other mourners. Again, those two conditions which lend themselves so admirably to the generation of primitive fears are present: childhood, and loneliness.

A lot of horror fiction relies heavily on people's basic fears. One of my own is unreasonable: I am quite happy walking along enveloped in thick mist or fog, but if I am on a hillside and I can see a bank of mist approaching, I am immediately fearful. As far as I know this is an uncommon fear, so if I used it as the basis for a horror novel it might not work too well; it would strike no universal chord.

But many fears *are* universal: being buried alive; being burned alive; sudden, complete paralysis; rats, spiders and snakes; falling helplessly through space; insanity. The use of any of these symbols or happenings will bring from your readers a predicatable response: a shudder, a chill of fear – and suspense created by the need to read on to see if the poor devil in the book survives the unimaginable.

Poe wrote about the deliberate entombment of an enemy in *The Cask of Amontillado*. The crime takes place deep in dripping catacombs, the setting intensifies the suspense and there is no finer depiction of that particular horror.

In *The Mask,* Dean R. Koontz (writing as Owen West) tells in his prologue of a child (again) trapped in a cellar (entombed), terrified of spiders, and eventually burned to death.

Place Characters in Inner-city Landscapes to Suggest Violence

Not all horror novels use Gothic settings, and some pretty gruesome crimes occur in books outside the horror genre. Although such crimes do occur in rural areas – Agatha Christie's Miss Marple books have used bucolic settings to great effect – painting a picture of lush meadows yellow with buttercups over which skylarks sweetly trill does not easily bring about an aura of suspense.

Inner cities, on the other hand, are urban battlefields waiting for yet another endless night.

> I circled the block, stopped at a hole in the wall on Eighth Avenue, stopped again at Joey Farrel's. I felt restless and combative and got out of there when the bartender said something that irritated me. I don't remember what it was . . . Then I was walking. I was on Ninth Avenue across the street from Armstrong's, walking south, and there was something hanging in the air that was putting me on guard. Even as I was wondering at the feeling, a young man stepped out of a doorway ten yards ahead of me.

© Lawrence Block 1981. Extract from *A Stab in the Dark* by Lawrence Block. Reproduced by permission of Orion Publishing Group Ltd.

Lawrence Block is an American author whose Matt Scudder mysteries are highly praised. Block knows New York, and his dark descriptions reek of authenticity and menace. If you are writing a novel using a city with which you are familiar, to increase the possibilities of suspense you need simply to visualize the most run-down area and – either in your imagination or in reality – place yourself there in the dead of night.

Once again you are using people's primitive fears to create an atmosphere: the rattle of a bin lid in a dark alley where tiny eyes glitter; footsteps behind you that move when you move, pause when you pause; boarded-up windows scrawled with red and yellow graffiti, flanked by littered doorways in deep shadow; the slow-moving car that follows you along the kerb; the voice that whispers at you from the tinted windows . . .

Or, as J.J. Marric (John Creasey) put it in *Gideon's Fire*:

The April evening was chilly without being cold. The moon had dropped behind the roof of the house opposite. A hum of sounds from the docks across the river became more audible now – and then Jarvis heard the click-click-click of a bicycle with a broken spoke, and was sure that his man was approaching . . .

Mary Higgins Clark uses Grand Central Station, New York, as the setting for the sinister scenes in *A Stranger Is Watching*. See how she creates this atmosphere:

He moved quickly down the stairs to the lower level of the station . . . He made sure no guard was looking . . . He made his way past sewer pipes to a sloping ramp that led into the depths of the terminal. His movements became quicker, furtive. Overhead, the station was bustling with the comings and goings of travellers. Here in this poorly lighted area the sounds were different: the throbbing of a pneumatic pump, the rumbling of ventilating fans, the trickle of water.

Starved cats slithered in and out of the darkened tunnel under Park Avenue.

It is interesting to note how the author has exaggerated the sinister aspects of a place that, in truth, is not intrinsically sinister. Although the villain makes his way past sewer pipes, most people would recognise them only as pipes and so the label 'sewer' has been put in for effect. In the same way pumps 'throb' (nervous heartbeat), fans 'rumble' (menacing imagery), water 'trickles' (somehow disturbing), and all the cats are 'starved'.

Use a Big-business Environment to Suggest Intrigue

If you have read widely – or indeed made intelligent observations of life – you will know that suspense is present everywhere. Rugged mountain scenery, a moonlit graveyard, a lamplit street where cobbles glisten in the rain – all of these are superbly evocative settings. And because readers nowadays are extremely knowledgeable, presented in the right way the world of big business with its glamour and intrigue will hum with tension.

On a deck high above the water, four gentlemen enjoyed drinks and managed small talk while waiting for a visitor . . . big business was at hand . . . Each of the four was the CEO of a large public corporation. Each corporation was in the Fortune 500 . . . The smallest had sales last year of six hundred million, the largest, four billion. Each had record profits, large dividends, happy stockholders, and CEOs who

earned millions from their performances . . . And now the
lawyers were after them.

In *The Runaway Jury*, John Grisham stages a courtroom battle for
survival that involves businesses too large for most readers to
imagine – but which they will be eager to read about – and an
activity each of us sees every day: cigarette smoking. In the book
the issue to be thrashed out in court is whether smoking ciga-
rettes causes lung cancer.

The passage quoted in a fragmentary way covers two pages. In
the complete text the author creates an opulent location, estab-
lishes the (surface) reputations of these rich men, details the
enormity of the sums involved – then throws in the hook: 'And
now the lawyers were after them.'

The suspense in this book is generated by the attempts of a
single juror (and an accomplice) to influence the other members
of the jury while keeping out of the rich men's clutches.

Make a Fashion/media Scene Suggest Sexual Tension

It's probably getting pretty close to the truth to say that, in
fiction at least, money and sex are the two most common
motives for all kinds of skulduggery. If 'obsess' is too strong a
word, then at least we can say with certainty that those two
things *concern* most of us for most of our lives. And if you write
about anything that strikes a chord with virtually the whole of
the human race, then you must stand a better than average
chance of success.

A lot of glamorous women writers have themselves achieved
that gloss through the money made writing about it. A glance at

a short passage from *Malice* by American author Danielle Steel reveals both sex and suspense:

> He made her some coffee when she arrived, and he had already set up. There was a huge white leather chair, and a white fox throw covering part of it, and all he wanted was for her to sprawl on it in her jeans, and white T-shirt. He made her untie her hair, and it fell over her shoulders lavishly, and then he exchanged the T-shirt for his own starched white shirt, and little by little he got her to unbutton it, but the shots were all very chaste and modest. And she was surprised by how much fun it was. He took her in a thousand poses, and he had great music on, and each shot was almost like a caress as he danced around her.

In all deliberate evocations of a particular environment, the simplest of props suffice to create a vivid picture in the imagination. Although readers know this is a studio, a white leather chair with a white fox fur thrown over it suggests wealth, and there is a deliberate comparison made by bringing in the jeans and white T-shirt.

The suspense is created by the girl's increasing drowsiness after drinking the coffee, the blurred realization in her mind – and therefore the reader's – that something is going on, without there quite being enough detail to be absolutely sure exactly what.

Before continuing, it is important to remember that the boost given to the creation of suspense by evocative settings is not confined to all-action thrillers, or bestselling blockbusters. Rugged scenery can suggest high adventure as effectively in

Cornwall or in Wales as in the High Andes and, as you will see in the next chapter, suspense in a business environment does not have to take place on Wall Street, Madison Avenue or in the financial areas of Frankfurt or London.

In Practice

You will begin painting the first washes of your setting in the first chapter, continue to add colour and life as the book progresses and, if it is done with care, throughout the book you will benefit from having your characters move in an environment or atmosphere within which suspense can flourish. This makes your task easier. The landscape is always there as a backdrop to the action, and your readers are conscious of it – are, indeed, completely mesmerized by it – without perhaps realizing that the environment is contributing to the undercurrent of tension.

As examples we have looked at:

- rugged scenery
- a Gothic atmosphere
- inner-city landscapes
- a big business environment
- a fashion/media scene

In these we have seen how well-known writers have cleverly used a few words to create an environment, and seen how the world they have created has helped them to build up a certain kind of suspense. Clearly, a book can advantageously make use of several different settings.

Hammond Innes placed one of his characters in a boat sailing the chill waters of the English Channel in a book about deep-sea salvage operations and fraud. Gerald Seymour's characters moved painfully across the arid landscape of Afghanistan at the time of the Russian occupation.

You may wish your hero to move across the globe, perhaps following the poisonous trail of a drugs cartel from the icy streets of Amsterdam and London to the sweltering heat of the Middle and Far East. Although the main source of suspense will be your hero's constant fear of detection by the drug barons and their cold-blooded hit-men, each different environment travelled through as he follows the drugs pipeline will offer different possibilities.

In *From Russia with Love,* James Bond fights for his life aboard the Orient Express, an environment fraught with far different dangers from those encountered at the Sussex nature clinic he attended in *Thunderball.* In each skilfully drawn location readers will have instinctively anticipated or imagined the various catastrophes that might befall the intrepid agent: in the former a deliberate push from the open door of the speeding train, apprehension and torture by sinister secret police, a battle to the death with knife and pistol in the claustrophobic atmosphere of a locked railway carriage; in the latter a fatal dose of a rare poison administered by hypodermic syringe or in the special slimming diet, violent strangulation by a patient gone suddenly berserk, or a bizarre death on or in one of the special mechanical contraptions designed to revitalize neglected muscles.

In just the same way, given an appropriate and convincing setting readers will expect a heroine to walk into a situation where seduction is inevitable, anticipate a tense courtroom battle, or be mentally cringing in the certainty that a young thug is going to pounce from the shadows of a dark, litter-strewn alley.

Paint the right picture, and readers will write the plot for you. And if they don't quite go that far, it will certainly make the next stage of your novel's construction that much easier.

2   Maximizing the Suspense Potential of Plot and Main Conflict

If the setting for your novel is the evocative backdrop against which your readers will see the story played out, then the main conflict – and the plot woven around it – are the bait and line that draw them into the story and tow them through increasingly choppy waters to the dramatic climax.

Although the angler's rallying cry is 'Taut lines!' the author's must be the reverse, for the more tangled the strands of the plot (short of a hopelessly ravelled mass), then the more opportunities there are to create suspense.

As we move through the various stages of creating suspense in fiction it will become increasingly obvious that the essential ingredients in the process are characters, and that the suspense in most situations is caused because readers are waiting for the outcome – waiting to find out either *what* will happen, *when* it will happen, or even *if* it will happen.

But a convoluted plot, on its own, is not enough. At each twist and turn the problems or conflicts encountered by the leading characters must be important enough – within the context – to have a disastrous effect on their lives if not tackled successfully, and it's the nature and role of the conflict in the creation of suspense in your novel that is dealt with here.

The dire warning given to aspiring thriller writers nowadays is that, because television and cinema audiences have seen and become inured to every form of violence, any book hoping for success must be concerned with events that threaten the very survival of the human race.

Of course, this is pure nonsense.

Nevertheless, all authors live in the modern world, and many do believe that, even when writing a straightforward romance or family saga, the conflicts must be of earth-shattering importance. The clue to why this is clearly not true lies in the three words of qualification used a little earlier in this introduction: 'within the context'.

If watching a millionaire sweat out the rescue of his beautiful daughter from Colombian kidnappers who have threatened to kill her creates suspense for one type of reader, the anxious moments experienced by an Accrington single mum when her 5-year-old daughter is late back from the corner shop will have another kind of reader on the edge of his seat.

Instead of writing always about cataclysmic events, a writer would be far better off writing about some happening with which a reasonable cross-section of the reading public can be guaranteed to empathize. So in this chapter we will look at how to:

- Instil fear
- Think life-and-death, money, and sex
- Embroil characters in seemingly impossible situations
- Create strongly opposing characters
- Plot – weave a tangled web

And, always, we will think in terms of context.

Instil Fear

If you look at fear in its very broadest sense, then it becomes obvious that to a greater or lesser degree most of the situations we face in life have within them an element of fear.

Every decision made by the millionaire whose daughter has been kidnapped will be activated by fear.

But a child starting school is frightened, and so is an old person entering a home for the aged. People living in poverty will be frightened that there is not enough money in the purse when they reach the supermarket check-out; a rich man might always have the fear of not appearing to be free enough with his money. A redundant executive going for an interview will be frightened of failure; an office junior, short on experience and intelligence, might be stricken with fear at sudden success in the form of promotion.

There are stories here, aren't there? Dozens. None of them is cataclysmic. All are based on fear. And they are simple fears. Everyday fears. Fears that your friends and your relatives will recognize and understand – because they will have experienced them, or others so similar that the very thought sends shivers down their spine.

Although the advice was to write about fears with which many of your readers will empathize, if you wish to go beyond that it is easy to intensify even the simplest of fears and so make any decision that has to be taken, or any result that must be achieved or attained, much more important, and heighten the suspense.

The child starting school can be ignored, for there will be insufficient experience to generate anything more than that most primitive of fears: fear of the unknown.

But what if an old lady entering a retirement home has heard ghastly tales of cruel treatment, even murder, at the hands of the owners – but nobody will believe her? The primitive fear of the unknown that is also present in this poor old lady is now intensified because, in addition to things she knows nothing about, there are some things about which she knows altogether too much.

It's almost a certainty that a redundant executive will have a hefty mortgage, an expensive car, perhaps private school fees to find each term and a cosy villa in Spain to maintain. But if you dig a little deeper you might find a family history of mental illness, and see signs of it in the executive's behaviour even before his fall from favour. And if that hereditary family madness has always manifested itself in the murder of loved ones, then when our executive goes for his interview he will be sweating blood (knowing that failure could easily tip him over the edge), and so will the readers.

Finally in this little discussion on instilling fear, let's come back down from the rather bizarre extremes we have been using as intensifiers and say that our young office boy who is so scared of promotion has a beautiful girlfriend who is openly demanding his success; limited intelligence makes it impossible for him to attain the giddy heights of a top salary, yet he knows he will lose her if he doesn't. . . .

Think Life-and-death, Money, and Sex

Because we've already glanced in passing at one life-and-death situation, let's look more closely at this most traumatic of conflicts.

One of the snippets of advice given to writers searching for ideas or plots is to think 'what if?', and if you apply that simple question again and again to our millionaire/Colombian kidnapper example it's easy to see how, with each step, the suspense can be cranked up to unbearable levels:

- What if the millionaire has no liquid assets when there is a huge ransom demand, and he must chase around to raise money?
- What if our millionaire is unpopular, and banks turn him away?

- What if the desperate millionaire decides to sweat it out, call the kidnapper's bluff?
- What if he is then sent the bloody tip of his daughter's finger, with the promise of more, unless. . . ?
- What if, when time is running out, he hires a couple of mercenaries and arranges a dangerous rescue attempt?
- What if the mercenaries take the millionaire's huge sum of borrowed cash up front, then disappear? Or take the cash, then kidnap the millionaire's wife? Or hold the millionaire to ransom?

A kidnapping is a glaring example of a life-and-death situation, and throughout any such story the suspense is derived from uncertainty over the outcome. The degree of suspense comes from the author's skill and originality when moving the story forwards through each successive stage.

Of course, life-and-death situations aren't confined to the deal-ings between kidnappers and millionaires. The Accrington single mum's worry for her daughter who is late returning from the corner shop can be stretched to tragedy and become the suspense-ful hunt for a murderer; the health of an old lady entering a retirement home can take a turn for the worse, the result being a hospital drama whose suspense is heightened when it is feared that her wayward son's flight from Australia will arrive too late.

The points in the example above are far from original. However, if you can pretend for a moment that there *is* someone out there who has not read such a story, then – if the author has, as a prerequisite, managed to generate in the reader some sympa-thy for the daughter or the millionaire – it is quite easy to imagine the effect each stage would have on them. And it would be a very good exercise to see if you can dream up improvements – six new steps – that replace the given examples and generate maximum suspense.

So far we have dealt in some detail with a life-or-death situation which also involves money.

Sex is the third subject of this section and, like the others, it has the potential for creating a high degree of suspense. It goes without saying that characters are necessary, and if we stick with the example we have been using then it's easy to see how the suspense can be heightened considerably if we have the kidnapped daughter becoming attracted by the young, handsome kidnapper.

That situation, like any other, could be arrived at by asking 'what if?' Other possibilities might be: 'What if the millionaire's wife takes all phone calls, and becomes sexually attracted to the kidnapper through hearing his strong, masculine voice?'; or, 'What if the police are involved and the millionaire becomes hopelessly distracted by his strong sexual attraction to a female detective?'; but the permutations really are limitless.

However, the sexual relationship we have chosen is that between kidnapper and kidnapped, and continual application of 'what if?' will give us a succession of answers to *what* will happen. What the question doesn't do is give us the answer to *when* it will happen, or *if* it will happen – and it is the readers' burning desire to find out those answers that will create suspense.

Embroil Characters in Seemingly Impossible Situations

If you look back you will see that when we were discussing our millionaire's problems I gave as a prerequisite for maximum effect the author generating in the reader some sympathy for the daughter or the millionaire. In the talk about instilling fear you will have seen an intense preoccupation with characters, their feelings and their fears, and this subject will be dealt with much more fully in Chapter Seven.

Putting likeable characters in impossible situations is guaranteed to create suspense, because readers feel for them and cannot imagine how they can extricate themselves. They know the hero is going to escape, and they know that there must be no fortuitous arrival of bugle-blowing cavalry or knight in shining armour. But when a man is hanging by his fingernails from a precipice in the middle of the night, miles from the nearest farm, buffeted by a gale – and with no handy mobile phone – then the problem looks insoluble, death seems inevitable . . . and turning just one more page of the book becomes irresistible.

For the writer, the joy of impossible situations is the suspense they create, and the satisfaction that comes from arriving at a solution. The purest examples of impossible situations are those mysteries where a murder victim is found alone in a room with the doors and windows locked on the inside.

If that is your forte, then go to it, because although the style might need to be brought up to date, traditional detective novels are perennial favourites and the sheer nature of the puzzle creates suspense.

But if we are to adhere to our principle (writing about happenings with which a reasonable cross-section of the reading public can be guaranteed to empathize) then we need to create impossible situations in the context of everyday events – and that's more difficult.

Let's look again at our office boy stricken by success.

This could be an interesting short novel for teenagers, and if we jump in some way into the story when our hero has been catapulted to the dizzy heights of assistant office manager (if such a position exists), then it will be an interesting exercise to invent a situation that grows progressively more complicated until it becomes impossible.

It might go something like this:

Competing businessman phones for appointment with boss.
It is Friday, and boss is out for the day.
Assistant Manager makes appointment for following week.
Puts phone down, remembers boss will be on holiday.
Short on brains, long on cheek, opts to take boss's place.
On the day, flustered, begins to create complications.
Hastily signs deals favouring competitor, bankrupting boss.
Dazed competitor questions assistant's authority.
Assistant blurts out that boss was taken ill, and died.
Competitor leaves office, informs journalist friend.

Already our office boy has dug himself into a deep hole. Things can be made progressively worse, or can be sorted out from that point – but wouldn't it be interesting to be a fly on the wall when the office boy talks to his girlfriend . . . and reads next day's newspapers!

Although several steps down the ladder, this farcical situation does fit into the big-business environment discussed in Chapter One. It is, moreover, a situation which will strike a chord with any readers who have been left on their own in charge of an office when their superior has been away.

Create Strongly Opposing Characters

When you compile a list of characters prior to writing your novel, or create them as you write, you must remember that friends who are so close that they are always in harmony will never be in conflict and so cannot contribute to suspense.

It is not unrealistic to suggest that, in a highly charged book written to create maximum tension and suspense, most of the

characters will be disagreeing – if not actually coming to blows –
for most of the time.

Start an argument, and you attract a crowd. Place two people
in opposition with daggers drawn, and you will make the air sing
with tension. Put the outcome of an altercation always in the
balance, and you create suspense.

If a man goes to his father for a loan to set him up in business,
don't have the father saying, 'Certainly, son how much do you
need?'

Instead, put angry words in his mouth, let him refuse point-
blank, say the scheme is crackpot and doomed to failure and ask
his son if he thinks he's made of money. In return the son will
certainly not say, 'Oh, well, sorry for bothering you, Dad', and
slink away, but instead will angrily point out that if it was his
brother doing the asking the father would be writing a cheque, he
has always favoured the younger sibling, even down to leaving
the bulk of the estate to him in his will . . . And, of course, the
mother will join in to make it a three-way tussle.

So far so good. But because characters in a book must always
act for a reason (or it will not ring true), then in order to have
father and son argue as a matter of course each and every time
either of them expresses an opinion, then they must be strongly
opposing characters.

This may not be the cleverest example to have chosen: most
parents and children *do* argue as a matter of course. But one
superb real-life example shows exactly what I mean – that of
Rudolph Nureyev and his father.

One was a Russian soldier who came back from the war a
changed man. The other was his son, a boy who wanted to
become a ballet-dancer. Can you imagine what they could possibly agree about when they met? Would those two people,
separated by age, experience and ambitions, have anything in
common?

In fact, they did have areas of sympathy, of course, for this was real life, not fiction; but if you place such diametrically opposed characters in your fiction the sparks will fly, you will have your work cut out trying to put words in their mouths that *don't* constitute argument – and your readers will always be in that suspenseful state of wondering (as they must be throughout your book) what on earth is going to happen next.

Plot – Weave a Tangled Web

A plot can be the straightforward, chronological unfolding of an adventure yarn, or it can be the complicated skeleton – or tangled web – that lies beneath the surface of a story and twists and turns and always keeps readers guessing; in other words, always keeps them in suspense.

So far, the closest we have come to writing a straightforward chronological plot has been the short experiment with the office boy who became an assistant manager and proceeded to ruin the firm. However, once we had introduced sexual complications into the affair of the millionaire's kidnapped daughter, we were on our way to weaving a tangled web.

A tangled web is highly effective for suspense purposes because it keeps readers guessing about several things at the same time. However, what we are talking about here is the various, interlocking strands of the main plot, not about sub-plots (which are dealt with in the next chapter). Deciding what constitutes plot and sub-plot can be a tricky business (and whether it's important to know the difference might be a good subject for debate!).

Let's say that, in my opinion, the extra complication of the kidnapped girl's infatuation with the young kidnapper is one more strand of a developing main plot. In the same way, we can increase the suspense still further by giving the kidnapper a blonde girlfriend who is his accomplice, and who becomes furiously jealous as she sees the kidnapper respond to his victim's amorous attention.

If we feel that it's time to think of something else other than sex, then you can recall what we discussed in the last section. All the characters will argue all the time, and in particular you will have the detectives on the spot arguing not only with each other, but with their superior who is controlling the investigation from HQ.

More strands in the developing main plot.

It would be possible – though not advisable unless you're writing a farce – to incorporate the other two sexual complications: the millionaire's wife failing for the kidnapper's voice, and the millionaire smitten by the delectable female detective.

You would now end up with (depending on which of the complications you have included):

Young girl held to ransom.

Millionaire decides to sweat it out.

He receives the severed tip of his daughter's finger.

He contacts two mercenaries.

Detectives consider changing methods – can't agree.

Meanwhile . . . wife is being seduced by the kidnapper's voice.

Daughter finds the kidnapper's personality sexually attractive.

Millionaire is becoming attracted to female detective.

Kidnapper's girlfriend is becoming dangerously jealous.

This is on a par with the situation our office boy dug himself into, and it's beginning to look as if I should be writing comedy. However, although these miniature plots are deliberately tongue-in-cheek, if each step is looked at in isolation then the serious suspense possibilities inherent in each situation become apparent.

In a genuine kidnapping, emotions run high and the various sexual tensions described would be potentially explosive; and perhaps the strangest thing about this deliberately risible attempt at complicated plotting is that all possible sexual permutations between victims, criminals, parents and detectives, have happened before, and will happen again.

And all of this is before we've added the complications of one or more sub-plots!

In Practice

The information given in the first four sections of this chapter is fairly straightforward, so I can safely leave you to get on with writing that book in which you are instilling fear; thinking life-and-death, money, and sex; embroiling characters in seemingly impossible situations; and creating strongly opposing characters.

But the process of creating a plot is quite another matter, and because a good plot is the strong skeleton on which the flesh of your story will be built up layer by layer, I think a bit more guidance is in order.

Clearly, all your plots will be different, and because you will have your own original ideas I cannot – and should not – attempt to write a plot for you. But there is one important principle that will help to make all your plots, if not clever, then certainly plausible. That principle is cause and effect.

People don't just do things – they do things *because* . . .

If you take some time to consider that statement, you will see that it applies to pretty well everything anybody does. Even if a man decides to take up indoor bowling, he will do it for a reason: he will go bowling because he has seen it on television, because he wants exercise, because he wants to socialize, or even simply because he is bored. What he won't do is wake up one morning and think, I know, I'll go bowling.

When you begin working out your plot, always think cause and effect. If we use our millionaire as an example, when his daughter is kidnapped, he will *react*. When the millionaire reacts, whatever he decides to do will involve the kidnappers, and they will *respond*, perhaps by stating new terms or setting a deadline. Once again, the millionaire (and the authorities) will *react*.

This sequence of cause and effect, of action and reaction, is essential for the building of a strong, plausible plot – and for the creation of suspense.

Suspense in the above story is created because at each action on the part of the kidnappers, readers will see no way out and will wonder how the millionaire can possibly react. When the distraught millionaire does react, readers will be on tenterhooks, wondering if what he has done will succeed, or fail. Early in the novel that reaction will certainly fail, creating an angry response from the kidnappers so that readers will see another critical dilemma confronting the millionaire, with the need for another desperate reaction . . .

Cause and effect creates plausible plots that build suspense, and keep readers turning the pages.

3 Entangling Plot and Sub-plot

In the last chapter I suggested that deciding when a plot becomes a sub-plot can be a tricky business. Now that we are into the chapter where sub-plot is our theme – and where we will be doing our best to add some knots and snarls to the existing webs we have created – it's important to explain the difference so that at the very least you know where you are when you start.

If you look at the people caught in our kidnapping web, you will see that although we have created other problems than the simple one of finding the victim/kidnapper, we have not moved off the main track. The millionaire wants to find his daughter, the mercenaries are recruited to do the job, the detectives are there to do the official business and the various sexual overtones are all between characters at the heart of the crisis.

So perhaps one way of describing the difference between plot and sub-plot is to say that everything occurring on the main line of our story is plot, anything that occurs on a branch line – and even offshoots of branch lines – that deviates from the main track is sub-plot.

In this chapter we will be covering:

- Creating tense, effective sub-plots
- How sub-plot conflict increases main-plot suspense
- Building thriller tension through linked sub-plots
- Using a sub-plot to intensify a romantic affair

Creating Tense, Effective Sub-plots

'The Affair of the Millionaire's Daughter' is developing along suitably dramatic lines, but our readers are becoming a bit jaded, and beginning to yawn and look at the clock. Since page one they have been bombarded with the troubles of the millionaire, his daughter, the kidnapper, an airy-fairy wife who should know better and a couple of detectives who are constantly at each other's throats. Some relief is needed, and although it doesn't have to be light (though a little levity can come in useful) it must be something that arouses fresh interest.

So, let's think branch line.

We've already got our lecherous millionaire giving the female detective constable the eye, and she is quite used to that. But she has also got serious troubles of her own. Our young detective constable has a 3-year-old daughter. The little girl is in hospital with a fever that could be meningitis or one of a number of other illnesses with similar symptoms. Whenever she's not on duty, Mummy is there sitting by the little girl's bed, talking to the doctors, talking by phone to the father who works in Manchester or nipping back to her flat to cook up a quick stir-fry.

This inchoate sub-plot has in it those elements that will naturally interest readers and create suspense: hospital, a child, a suspected serious illness. But, please note, only 'suspected': because anything definitely diagnosed would take away some of the suspense.

You will notice that in addition to creating new complications, our branch line (sub-plot) also introduces new characters. This is where you must keep tight control, because if you start getting involved with the nurses and doctors who are looking after the little girl, then you will be moving too far from your original plot and, in effect, writing a different book.

Can we do a similar sub-plot manipulation with the young man falling over himself to bankrupt the firm?

Thinking branch line again, perhaps the young assistant manager sends a secretary into the boss's office to jot down the appointment in his diary. While in there she uses the telephone to call her mother, telling her that she'll be late home that night, and making some excuse. Actually, she is starting a new part-time job serving behind the bar at the Mop and Bucket, but knows her mother won't approve.

That sounds fine, comfortably in line with the lighter tone of this story's main plot. The small suspense element can be increased if we show the girl worrying about the job because she has never done anything like it before and is painfully shy (think of how people will naturally behave, react).

But if we want to build maximum suspense into our story we should go for something more dramatic. Obviously every plot/sub-plot variation can't revolve around a medical drama, so try to think of another kind of potential crisis that must be averted (perhaps inventing a different character) which is apposite, but which – because we are discussing sub-plot – must have nothing to do with the main plot.

Perhaps, after listening to the rival businessman's news about the sudden death, the reporter pops into a restaurant for lunch with a lawyer. He has written a freelance article about the royals, and is being sued . . .

How Sub-plot Conflict Increases Main-plot Suspense

It is quite a good plan to write a simple novel with an outstanding main plot and a couple of sub-plots that have their own, satisfying mini-climaxes. Done this way you create a clearly defined structure that ensures readers are totally involved with the main conflict, while providing a couple of side-shows to keep their interest from flagging in the inevitable flat spots.

But you can do much better than that. In addition to having your sub-plots act as interesting but unconnected diversions, you can use them to enhance and make more acceptable certain existing features of the main plot; and you can, over a period of time, cause them to have a profound effect on the way the main plot develops and climaxes.

Let's look back at 'The Saga of the Seized Socialite'. We devised an interesting sub-plot revolving around the sick daughter of the detective constable. On its own that provides a great deal of additional interest, and creates a lot of suspense.

But giving the detective constable a sick daughter has placed her under stress. Readers can now see a reason for the tense arguments between the two detectives. They will start to feel understanding and compassion for the constable, resentment and dislike for the male detective sergeant who doesn't understand. That's one bonus that has come directly from a simple sub-plot.

The second bonus comes if you decide that your delightful little sub-plot is going to have a direct bearing on the main story. Indeed, it can do this already simply by having the stress the detective constable is under cause her to make a tragic mistake with far-reaching consequences.

But a far better way is to link the sub-plot to the main plot and, after a time, draw the two strands together so that as the denouement approaches they are running in tight parallel – but still apart – until, at the moment of supreme climax, everything comes together and all is revealed to readers and to those characters who have – for the purposes of suspense – been kept in the dark.

And what better way to achieve this in the plot and sub-plot under discussion than to have the nurse who is deeply involved with the sick child be the devoted sister of the kidnapper?

This is suspense unlimited, which can be developed in a

number of ways. For example, the readers know of the link between nurse and kidnapper, but the other 'goodies' in the book do not. So you will have the detective constable, in her most vulnerable moments, letting slip pieces of information about the case which the nurse then passes on to her brother (for, of course, she does not know he is the kidnapper). The kidnapper will of course react to each piece of information, and as the detective constable becomes more and more puzzled about the kidnapper's apparently telepathic reading of the situation, it will gradually dawn on the nurse that she is the leak, and the only person she is talking to is – her brother. Does she give him away?

An alternative way of handling the situation is for the nurse to be an accomplice who learns of her brother's mistreatment of the hostage through conversations with the detective constable, and gradually comes to realize that what they are doing is terribly wrong. The dilemma is the same: does she betray him?

By using either alternative – or a superior version you dream up yourself – the suspense now comes not only from watching the authorities and/or mercenaries close in on the kidnapper, but from the riveting sub-plot which has intense emotional overtones as the detective constable realizes what she has done and the nurse struggles with a wrenching decison.

Building Thriller Tension Through Linked Sub-plots

We have already looked at a couple of ways in which a sub-plot can link to the main plot to create suspense. Now we can examine how sub-plot linked to sub-plot further increases the suspense and keeps readers enthralled, and on their toes.

If you are not fed up to the back teeth with hearing about the weary cast in our kidnapping saga, we'll use that again because we have a ready-made plot/sub-plot that can be tweaked here and there to demonstrate what can be achieved by further subbing and linking.

In my own novel writing I start with the barest smidgen of an idea and no outline, and the reason this works (for me) is that situations develop from characters; there is that familiar pattern of cause and effect, of people doing something *because* . . .

I have already demonstrated that people rarely, if ever, do things in real life for no reason at all, and although it's often dangerous to equate fiction to real life, fictional characters must behave in a realistic and believable way.

So, if our detective constable is letting information slip to the nurse at the hospital, the other police officers on the case are going to look suspiciously at each other when the kidnapper seems to develop second-sight. As, in our saga, there is only the detective sergeant – and he knows *he's* not leaking information – he will suspect his colleague, inform his superior officer, and on his advice start feeding the unsuspecting detective constable false information. This will subtly change the tone of the meetings between constable and sergeant, and will involve new meetings between sergeant and superior which, because we stick to our principle of creating strongly opposing characters, will be acrimonious as one or the other strives to impose his will and direct the course of the investigation.

A linked sub-plot has been created. For our first sub-plot we created a detective sergeant/seriously ill daughter crisis. To link it to the main plot we decided that the nurse would be the kidnapper's sister. For our second sub-plot we added the detective sergeant/superior officer, linked that pairing to the detective constable/nurse, and complicated the nurse/kidnapper link by having her pass false information.

We still have a couple of main characters who can, if necessary, become involved in sub-plots. But it's as well to inject a cautionary note here. Too many sub-plots can confuse readers, and cause writers to get hopelessly lost. So if you are writing a short novel (fifty to sixty thousand words), write in no more than two simple sub-plots. In longer novels – a hundred thousand words and up – you will have much more room to work, and books of this length may *need* several sub-plots to sustain interest and add sufficient complexity to the plot.

Instead of putting any more pressure on the tormented millionaire, let's turn to his wife. We know she is attracted to the kidnapper, and we can perhaps excuse this if we make her a somewhat distant step-mother and therefore much less concerned for the kidnapped girl's welfare. So, how can we involve the wife in a sub-plot that can be linked to another sub-plot and then linked to the main plot?

I pointed out that characters in your book must, to a certain extent, behave naturally. They will respond in an expected way to stimuli, will react to situations according to human nature. If Molly Millionaire finds herself sexually attracted to a kidnapper, this will so appal her that she will at first strive to keep her dark feelings secret, then want desperately to share them and receive some reassurance that she is not a monster.

So . . . while the readers are kept in suspense as the main investigation continues to be thwarted by the clever kidnapper, the little girl recovers slightly only to relapse. The worried detective constable passes valuable information to the kidnapper's sister under the covert scrutiny of the detective sergeant. The superior officer plans how to trap the kidnapper by feeding him false information.

The millionaire's wife begins talking to a woman journalist, a close friend, her sole aim being to unburden her soul. But in the process she unwittingly drops valuable clues (regional accent, likes and dislikes, background noises) that begin to suggest to the journalist the possible identity of the kidnapper, and even his location. She begins talking to her editor . . .

Using a Sub-plot to Intensify a Romantic Affair

With its emphasis on suspense this book will constantly be discussing that technique as applied to taut, pacy thrillers but, as was pointed out in the introduction, suspense is a vital element of every novel, whatever the genre. In the next chapter you will find a brief example of how a simple prologue technique can be used at the beginning of a romantic novel, and it's worth looking now at the way sub-plots can be used in much the same way as they were in the kidnapping saga to add interest, and suspense, to books with a romantic theme.

Many Mills & Boon romances feature a young girl flying off to a Caribbean island or the Australian bush, to take up employment with a rich family. The simplest idea has the girl arriving at her exotic/primitive new surroundings, falling madly in love with the handsome scion of the family, fighting to win him from the attractive existing girlfriend, succeeding only to find herself (for one reason or another) disgraced, fighting back, proving herself to have been wronged, marrying the scion and living happily ever after.

The suspense element throughout is of the 'will she/won't she' kind, and can be intense. That standard formula plot works well on its own, but can be spiced up with the addition of interesting sub-plots which closely follow those already discussed.

Again going on the principle of cause and effect, of characters acting in a certain way *because*, you might have the lonely young girl turning naturally to a distinguished older man for companionship and intelligent conversation because he reminds her so much of her father. However, this older man has been a notorious philanderer, and his wife quickly becomes jealous.

On its own this sub-plot would be an interesting diversion, perhaps leading to the older man's separation from his wife but a lifelong friendship with our heroine. But more suspense can be created by linking this sub-plot to the conflicts in the main plot – the struggle of the new girl on the block to win the love of the handsome heir – and you could do this in several ways.

The most obvious is for the jealous wife to begin spreading rumours about the relationship between her husband and the girl. The husband's reputation would give the rumours weight, and the young girl would find herself under a dark cloud of suspicion.

Another way of doing it would be to keep the jealousy simmering, but have the mature man a past lover of the hero's existing girlfriend, and still her close friend (and accomplice). He has befriended the heroine for the sole purpose of digging up something from her past that can be used against her.

There are endless permutations. More sub-plots can be added, they can be linked to the main plot and, as you will have seen, they are simple to create, make your job as a writer much more interesting – and have within them enormous suspense potential.

Having seen how sub-plots can be hatched, you are probably bursting with far more original ideas than those I have used as examples. But we have reached the stage now that someone rather famous once called not the beginning of the end, but the end of the beginning: you have finished what I call the preparatory work, and are about to begin the writing.

In Practice

By devising entertaining sub-plots you can create additional and separate suspense, or add to the complexity of the main plot when they are linked. But there are several areas where caution must be exercised.

Remember that a sub-plot must always be subordinate to the main plot. If a sub-plot becomes too strong, it will reduce the suspense being generated by the main plot, and become of equal value. When that happens, your readers will not be delighted at getting two plots for the price of one, but confused over which one they should be following.

Some sub-plot characters will be involved in the main action. You will naturally create secondary characters for them to meet within the sub-plot, but those must not be fully developed. If you start delving into *their* backgrounds and relationships, you have gone too far.

To create sub-plots that are entirely separate from a main plot, think of a railway branch line that leads off the main track; it will run parallel, but it will have no further connection.

To create linked sub-plots, think of a railway branch line that runs parallel to the main track, but has one or more additional connections further along the route. In your story, a main-plot character will be involved in the sub-plot, but those additional connections will be made by a secondary character, usually without the knowledge of the main-plot character.

4   Using the Prologue to Build Suspense

A prologue is often used by novelists, sometimes as a convenient way of giving information about prior events, often as a device to provide a tantalizing glimpse of what the book is about without giving away too many details.

That glimpse is the first chance the novelist has to inject suspense into his story, and to heighten the immediate effect a prologue is frequently written in vague terms. Readers must be hooked very early in a book, or they will be lost. A cleverly written prologue does that job admirably by setting out to tell readers something, then stopping just when it begins to get interesting. It is also the ideal tool for enabling the author to give information that – if put off until a later chapter – might slow the pace of the story and reduce suspense.

One of the questions that might occur to you is this: why do writers decide to use a prologue instead of getting on with things by going straight into the first chapter?

My own view of this is that despite the flexibility you have when writing a novel, most are written in a conventional way with narrative and dialogue and very little authorial intrusion; readers like to feel that they are living the story, rather than having it related to them by a third person.

A prologue need take no note of any of these conventions. In the same way that an epilogue wraps up the tale, the prologue prepares; it is part of the story, yet something set apart. The author can talk directly to readers, often imparting complex medical or technical information in a straightforward way. If done in the novel proper, there would be the need to resort to dialogue which might appear false, or forced, or authorial intrusion in the middle of a good story.

In order to achieve the most dramatic effect, when you write your prologue you should try to:

- Cloak it in mystery
- Make it suggestive
- Leave much unexplained

You will not be able to do all of those things in each prologue you write. In some you will mention names, in others you will do a lot of explaining and by so doing make the main conflict fairly obvious. But if you retain some of the mystery, and all of the suggestiveness, you will have aroused the interest of most of those who read the prologue to its conclusion.

Cloak It in Mystery

This is the story of a lovers' triangle, I suppose you'd say – Arnie Cunningham, Leigh Cabot, and, of course, Christine. But I want you to understand that Christine was there first. She was Arnie's first love, and while I wouldn't presume to say for sure (not from whatever heights of wisdom I've attained in my twenty-two years, anyway), I think she was his only true love. So I call what happened a tragedy.

© Stephen King 1983. Extract from *Christine* by Stephen King. Reproduced by permission of Hodder and Stoughton Ltd.

Those are the opening lines of the prologue to the horror novel written by the American author Stephen King. After those seventy-three words – which inhabit their own separate paragraph – the prologue goes on for a further two and a half pages in which the author carefully delineates the character of the tragic hero and to a lesser extent that of the story's narrator.

The bulk of this prologue was probably written by Stephen King to get those character descriptions out of the way and leave the author free to get on with the story when the first chapter begins. When he does so, he will have no need to resort to literary devices such as flash-backs, or strain to present character descriptions through the eyes of other characters.

But the main effect of this prologue as far as we are concerned is to create suspense, and that effect is achieved by being craftily misleading in those first few lines.

The book is called *Christine*. Christine is mentioned in the prologue's opening paragraph, and then left alone. The natural assumption is that she is a girl, but those of you who have read the book will know that to assume that would be wrong. Christine herself is cloaked in mystery, and the mystery is deepened when Stephen King's narrator (not named) mentions a tragedy which must surely be linked to the lovers' triangle.

Suspense is created in a similar way in the following extract from the prologue to *From Potter's Field* by Patricia Cornwell, but there are much more sinister overtones:

Toward the Ramble [in Central Park, New York], rocks were black beneath stars, and he could hear and see his breathing because he was not like anybody else. Temple Gault had always been magical, a god who wore a human body. He did not slip as he walked, for example, when he was quite certain others would, and he did not know fear.

. . . He set an old army knapsack in the snow, and held his bare bloody hands in front of him . . .

... He washed his hands and face in soft new snow, then patted the used snow into a bloody snowball . . .

Oh, there is mystery here all right. Temple Gault is magical, a man not like other men, a god in human form. But this god has bloody hands, he carries an army knapsack (surely not empty?), he is digging in the snow in New York's Central Park and, later in this quite short prologue, we see him scraping the snow away from a hatch, opening it, and dropping down into the New York subway.

In these prologues, two different authors have teased their readers by presenting characters cloaked in mystery. In the first, Stephen King cunningly created a situation in which one character is, quite naturally, assumed to be something 'she' most definitely is not. In the second, Patricia Cornwell has sparingly painted a chilling situation through a man's actions, and used straightforward exposition to tell us that this man is different from other men – without, of course, telling us why.

With her mention of blood and the suggestion of violent murder, Patricia Cornwell has created suspense by reaching out and touching the primitive that is present in all of us. Many authors use this method, and the prologue to *Morning Glory*, by LaVyrle Spencer, is particularly effective.

It begins with a train pulling into the station in Whitney, Georgia, where a black carriage with covered windows awaits its arrival. A young woman alights from the train. She has a baby in her arms. As she steps down from the train she is met by a grim man garbed in black. Timidly, she says hello to him. He is her father. She is escorted to the waiting carriage, and from the conversation between the young woman and her father, and the harsh words spoken by her own mother when she and the baby reach the carriage, it becomes clear to readers that the young woman is not married.

From the railway station, the young woman and her baby are taken home, quickly escorted inside by her black-garbed mother, and a green shade is pulled down to cover the windows.

The clincher to this stunning prologue comes in the final lines:

> The young mother was never seen leaving the house again, nor were the shades ever lifted.

© LaVyrle Spencer 1989. Extract from *Morning Glory* by LaVyrle Spencer. Reproduced by permission of HarperCollins Publishers Ltd.

Make It Suggestive

Although this next quotation is not labelled a prologue by its author, it performs exactly the same function. It is taken from *Children of Tender Years*, by Ted Allbeury.

> The way we selected out victims was as follows: we had two SS doctors on duty at Auschwitz to examine the incoming transports of prisoners. These would be marched by one of the doctors, who would make spot decisions as they walked by. Those who were fit to work were sent into the camp. Others were sent immediately to the extermination plants. Children of tender years were invariably exterminated since by reason of their youth they were unable to work.
> *Part of a sworn deposition made at Nuremburg dated 5th April 1946 by SS Obersturmführer Rudolf Hess, Commandant of Auschwitz.*

There is very little mystery in this opening. It is extremely explicit, clear enough in its message to chill any readers' blood and make them wonder what horrors await them if they read on.

The high suspense in this kind of opening is created by appealing to human compassion. Acts of indescribable horror are here described, and because part of that last sentence has been chosen as the title, the suggestion is that the plight of those children is the theme running through the book.

But the introductory passage is suggestive without giving anything away; and because, unlike in the previously quoted examples, there is no mention of characters or the mood and content of the book, it is all the more intriguing. It is quite possible that the author is merely quoting a passage from history to explain where he got the title – then telling a story about a nursery school in the heart of England. He might be using the term to suggest that all adults are, in times of high crisis, reduced to childlike behaviour, and then go on to write a thriller set in modern-day America.

This is part of the beauty of making your prologue suggestive. A suggestion leads to an assumption, and in order to find out if their assumptions are correct, readers must read on – often, as in the case of *Christine*, to encounter nail-biting suspense and discover that at least one of their assumptions was wrong.

Much the same method used by Ted Allbeury was chosen by Michael Gilbert in the prologue (again not labelled as such) to *The Night of the Twelfth*. Gilbert uses Thomas Gray's 'Ode on a Distant Prospect of Eton College':

Alas, regardless of their doom,
The little victims play!
No sense have they of ills to come
Nor care beyond today:
Yet see how all around 'em wait
The ministers of human fate
And black Misfortune's baleful train.
Ah, show them where in ambush stand
To seize their prey the murtherous band,

Ah, tell them, they are men!

Because of its antiquity, and the language it uses, this passage seems much less explicit that the one chosen by Ted Allbeury. Yet although it was written in 1747 it addresses a fear very much in today's news. The mention of 'little victims' and 'men'is extremely suggestive. The picture evoked will raise righteous indignation, and few readers will be able to resist the urge to read on.

In the prologue to *Tremor*, Winston Graham forsakes quotations and uses his own outstanding powers of description to tell us how the earth came into existence, and something of its structure. He then goes on to explain how and why earthquakes occur, and mentions famous earthquakes such as that in San Francisco in 1906 and the 1923 earthquake in Japan that killed more than one hundred thousand people.

He then homes in on the Agadir earthquake of 1960. He quotes statistics: twelve thousand people were killed, among them British and Americans.

The novel is set in 1960. The hero of the book is a young British writer. He is on his way to Agadir . . .

In the same way, in the prologue to *Fever*, Robin Cook uses cold, clinical medical description to detail the way benzene has entered a body and progressed from the bloodstream to bone marrow. The prologue suggests that this invasion might have been harmless were it not for the presence of a rogue cell, which has part of its DNA damaged by the chemical and so begins to divide, rapidly producing more damaged cells.

Finally, as with the prologue to *Morning Glory*, the last paragraph delivers the blow that will chill readers' hearts and create enormous suspense:

It was the beginning of an aggressive, acute myeloblastic leukaemia in the body of a twelve-year-old girl, starting on

December 28. Her name was Michelle Martell, and she had no idea what was wrong except for a single symptom: she had a fever!

© Robin Cook 1982. Extract from *Fever* (Macmillan, 1982).

Of course, this method of creating suspense in the prologue by the use of suggestion relies heavily on ordinary people's fears, and this is dealt with much more fully in Chapter Eleven. Suffice it to say here that people of a certain age will remember the horrors of the Second World War; people of all ages see the tragic results of similar atrocities flashing across our television screens today; earthquakes are an all too frequent occurrence the results of which are brought home to us through the same medium and, of course, all of us at some time in our lives know of somebody stricken with an incurable illness.

Leave Much Unexplained

It will be fairly obvious that if too much is given away in the prologue, suspense will be destroyed and readers will be lost. Indeed, the techniques of cloaking it in mystery and making it suggestive both have as a prerequisite the need to leave virtually everything to the readers' imagination; and when you are creating suspense, it is the reader's imagination that is working overtime with you, making it all possible.

I had originally intended to recommend leaving the names of characters out of the prologue, but I now feel that in many ways putting the names in helps create suspense. The extract from *Christine* is one obvious example, and if you can get your readers interested in a character that early in the story – indeed, before the story has started then whatever startling events have been hinted at will have been personalized, and become more effective.

In Practice

Writers of romances will immediately see the possibilities in Stephen King's method. He openly stated the theme of the book, went on in the rest of the prologue to describe the two main characters in great detail, but said nothing about the mysterious 'Christine'.

Many of your stories can be opened with a similar prologue. To whet their appetites, give readers a reasonable idea of what the book is about. To create suspense, leave one character cloaked in mystery:

Jane knew as soon as tall, handsome Mark Grainger sat next to her on the plane that something would happen between them on this Caribbean holiday. Openly seeking romance, throughout the flight she went out of her way to be at her sparkling, effervescent best. Mark's response was warm beyond her wildest dreams, and it would have been a magical start to a holiday had it not been for the strange behaviour of the beautiful stewardess . . .

From that point such a prologue can be finished quite quickly, or expanded to include as many tantalizing glimpses of the book as you feel necessary to build suspense.

That same prologue needs very little alteration to make it suitable for the introduction to a mystery novel:

Chief Inspector Doyle knew as soon as the uncouth detective sergeant sat next to him on the plane and ordered a Jack

Daniels on the rocks that this Caribbean assignment was going to tax his patience. Openly seeking peace and quiet in which to marshal his thoughts for the task ahead, throughout the flight he was subjected to an endless stream of bawdy tales that would have made a rugby veteran blush. It would have been a disastrous start to an already difficult overseas assignment had it not been for the strange behaviour of the elderly German seated across the aisle. Had he seen him before? Doyle couldn't be sure. All he knew was . . .

Many books can be opened with an intriguing, suggestive quotation. Ted Allbeury's was about war, but a spy novel can draw on a wide library of quotations from the war and Cold War years, and others that have their origins elsewhere but are still apposite. F. Scott Fitzgerald wrote the following (in *The Crack-up*, published posthumously in 1945), and it might well be used as an intriguing short prologue to a book in which the main character turns out to be a double agent:

The test of a first rate intelligence is the ability to hold two ideas in the mind at the same time, and still retain the ability to function.

Detective stories might open with quotations from the police records of the country in which they are set, and in the writings of Indians of the American West there are many dignified statements that will grace – and add suspense to – the prologue of any book with that setting:

Hear me, Lakotas . . . before the ashes of the council fire are cold, the Great Father is building his forts among us. You have heard the sound of the white soldiers' ax upon the Little Piney. His presence here is an insult and a threat. It is an insult to the spirits of our ancestors. Are we to give up their sacred grounds to be plowed for corn? Lakotas, I am for war.

Those were the words spoken by the great Lakota chief, Red Cloud, in 1866. There is no need for me to go into details about the particular events those words presaged. In them, there is the same inevitability as in the Nazi statement used by Ted Allbeury. They would make a stunning, suspenseful prologue to a novel that might be fiction based on fact, or all fiction, and indeed might have nothing at all to do with American Indians but merely be using that quotation to make an analogy.

They also provide a most suitable transition into the next chapter.

5 The First Chapter – Suspense Starts Here

Many aspiring writers of novels relying heavily on suspense frequently hear the advice to 'start with a bang'. They then pop along to their local library and see on the shelves thrillers that open like a senior citizen's midsummer outing to Blackpool: interesting, yes, with lots of potential, true – but hardly conducted at breakneck speed.

It's true that there are thrillers that start at a leisurely pace. But the aim of unpublished writers is to get a book accepted, the aim of published writers is to increase their sales, and to achieve either of those aims I would point to the example of two of Jack Higgins' books.

Exocet begins with a demonstration by army personnel of how easy it is to break into Buckingham Palace. There is some violence, a lot of suspense, and it is covered in six pages. *Solo* opens with the brutal murder of a businessman, by a criminal known as 'The Cretan' who is immediately revealed to be a world famous concert pianist. This opening is handled in four pages.

Both books are bestsellers, and they achieved high sales not just because of a stunning opening, but because they are rattling good reads. But the opening *is* important, and this chapter gives guidance on:

- Putting suspense into the first line
- Introducing the main character
- Establishing the setting and mood

- Hinting at the conflict
- Building suspense with scene reversal

Putting Suspense Into the First Line

Even if you have already written a prologue, the first chapter is where your book begins. The prologue – if it exists – is an appetizer, a teaser; it poses questions that go unanswered, promises intrigue and excitement without disclosing details.

Each one of the previous chapters has in one way or another laid the foundations for what is to come, but any notes or jottings that came out of them were for you alone. They are the raw materials that will lie hidden, but which will be manipulated by you to weave the tangled web that is your story. Now you must begin that story, and in order to entice your readers to turn the second page – and press on to the next chapter – you must capture their attention with the first.

> I inherited my brother's life. Inherited his desk, his business, his gadgets, his enemies, his horses and his mistress. I inherited my brother's life, and it nearly killed me.

© Dick Francis 1989. Extract from *Straight* (Michael Joseph, 1989). Reproduced by permission of Penguin Books Ltd.

Those are the first lines of the thriller written by Dick Francis. Three lines, to be exact, and if I am to stick strictly to the promise of this section, then I should point only to the first line. But if you look back you will see that, in just five words, even that says enough to capture the average reader's interest.

> Gordon Michaels stood in the fountain with all his clothes on.

© Dick Francis 1982. Extract from *Banker* (Michael Joseph, 1982). Reproduced by permission of Penguin Books Ltd.

The very first line of *Banker*.

What those outstanding first lines do is put one or more questions into readers' minds. In the first example, the immediate reaction is to ask, 'How?' In the second the question that springs to mind is, 'Why'? And I would suggest that what the author has done with both of these examples is to set his readers thinking and arouse their interest without, at this juncture, creating a high degree of suspense.

What we must strive to do with our first line – if at all possible – is to pose questions, but make them the kind of questions that have within them a degree of suspense, and so raise the tension. We want to perplex our readers, but we also want to frighten them; to make them uneasy; or, to use our definition of tension, we must attempt to create in our readers a small degree (because this is only the first line) of mental strain, excitement – and fear.

As the sound came again she stepped out onto the landing, trembling, and somewhere below her in the dark, empty house, a door creaked open.

In the examples taken from the work of Dick Francis I suggested that the questions posed were 'How?' and 'Why?'. But in this made-up first sentence the reader is faced with several altogether different questions, any one of which, if considered seriously, is likely to cause the hairs on the nape of the neck to bristle.

What is going on in this dark, supposedly empty house? If it is empty, *who* opened the door? Is she really alone in the house – and if not, and there is a stranger down there in the darkness, *what* should our heroine do?

And, of course, because finding the answer to all of those questions is intriguing, time-consuming, and likely to send shivers down the spine, with that first line you have achieved the desired effect: the suspense has created tension, and you have forced your reader to read on.

Introducing the Main Character

The primary reason for introducing the main character early in your story is because, in order to create suspense and tension, you must give your readers someone with whom they can identify. Although the lines I have written above are in themselves disturbing, they will not become truly frightening until the readers know more about the woman who has stepped out onto the landing.

A crude way of emphasizing this truth is to point out the depth of feeling aroused when a close relative is involved in a car crash, compared with the relative lack of feeling when the accident victim is a stranger.

Even giving the girl on the landing a name – Laura – will subtly increase a reader's involvement. Describe her as having dark hair, a pale face and huge, haunted eyes and readers are now becoming concerned. Impart the information that behind her in the bedroom, peacefully asleep, is her three-week-old baby daughter, and you not only introduce another potential, helpless victim, but also give Laura an air of maternal vulnerability which immediately arouses the readers' compassion.

While it is possible to create suspense in the first lines of your story, revealing anything of depth about your main characters will take time. Characters must be revealed slowly, and in the first chapter what you do reveal about your characters must be selected carefully, with much thought given to creating the maximum dramatic effect on your readers. Even when introducing characters, your mind should be on suspense.

Morgan Keen had caught that hesitation. He was thirty yards away across the yard, shirt-sleeved and sweating, stacking the last of the split logs inside the dim, sweet-smelling barn.

The beat of hooves had been carried to him on the rising wind as he swung the long-handled axe. He'd thought at first it was Grant, but the boy was checking fences to the south and this rider was coming from the direction of town. Morgan's grey eyes had narrowed as he watched the horseman approach. When he recognized Seeger his face hardened, and he straightened to his full height and ran strong fingers through his mane of iron-grey hair.

And even then, knowing none of the reasons for Seeger's visit, he thought of Adam, his elder son.

Ten lines or so from the second page of my own Western novel, *Bury Him Deep, in Tombstone*. And without any intrusion or crude divulging of information by the author, readers have learned a great deal about the main character. They know his name. From that, and from some of his actions and reactions, they will deduce that he is a tough man. He works hard, and looks after his property (the 'sweet-smelling barn'). He is neither young nor old ('iron-grey hair'); married, with just two sons ('elder', not 'eldest'); probably intelligent, certainly perceptive – his face has hardened, so the presence of the man called Seeger suggests bad news.

And he is a man who cares for his family. With the arrival of bad news, his first thoughts are for his boys. The undisclosed nature of that news – and Keen's reactions – introduce the element of suspense.

Establishing the Setting and Mood

It doesn't take a man with the perception of Morgan Keen to notice that the author has revealed much more in that opening than vague details about the main character. Readers have also gained an insight into the characters of Keen's two sons. One is hard at work checking fences; the other is, well, likely to be in trouble.

But for the purpose of this section it's interesting to see how, while getting on with the story, the author has begun creating a setting, and establishing the mood. Morgan Keen is working on his ranch. The rising wind suggests the approach of a storm. And in the arrival of Seeger there is the suggestion that a storm of a different kind is soon to break over the Keen ranch, so the mood is sombre, and electric with impending danger.

This mood that you establish in the first chapter sets the mood for the whole book. Any attempt to change it will disenchant your readers, and they will stop reading. You have already seen how settings have associations, their mere mention putting into the minds of readers a clear expectation of what is to come. So the setting of your book is a valuable tool to be used to start to build suspense. It should be chosen with care, and painted with painstaking skill.

That afternoon, so many years ago, the wind was whipping in off the harbour in sharp flurries, carrying with it icy salt spray to mingle with the smell of fish and machine oil; and raucously, insistently, like a harsh counterpoint to the gentle accents of the Oban fishermen, always there were the cries of those soaring, wheeling gulls.

That example is taken from my short story 'All the Colours of the Rainbow'. The setting is clear, has even been named. The mood has not been so obviously stated but, if you agree with me, then I think you will feel a suggestion of melancholy, or sadness; emotions that are, perhaps inherent in the mournful cry of sea birds.

At nine he listened to the chimes of Big Ben and the BBC news, learned nothing, switched off and stamped out onto the veranda. And he remained there for the next hour, brooding, always half-listening to the myriad sounds of a Mediterranean night: the soft sighing of the breeze, the distant chirping of crickets; the lazy mosquito hum of a plane on its fight path over Marbella, the sudden explosion of sound as the pilot nursed it to a feather-light touchdown then applied reverse thrust to avoid plunging into the sea from the end of the tongue of land that was the runway of Gibraltar airport.

This contrasting example is taken from the start of my unpublished thriller *The Tangier Crossing*, and again I have deliberately and in some detail established the setting. The mood is not so clear, but there is a hint of anger, and the unknown protagonist is obviously impatiently waiting for . . . something.

What that something is, what problems the protagonist is about to face, we do not know, so there is suspense, and there is tension. But no matter how clever authors may be, there is a limit to the amount of information that can be divulged in the first few lines of the first chapter.

Hinting at the Conflict

Although it has been suggested that there should be an attempt to give readers some knowledge of the conflicts facing the protagonist as early as the first page, or page and a half, of a short story, in a novel the author will have more time. Nevertheless, to ensure that the suspense created with so much effort in the first few lines is not only maintained but, to a certain extent, explained, hinting at the nature of the conflict should be one of your priorities. One way it can be done is demonstrated in this example from my short story 'Fifth Time Dead' (published in *The Alfred Hitchcock Mystery Magazine*).

> She'd been with him three weeks. This was the first time I'd called her.
> 'He got off,' I said when she answered. Her voice was husky, her breath so close to my ear my skin tingled all the way down to my hip. 'They called it an accident, so now he's taken my girl and killed my brother and got away with it both times.'

Dialogue has always been one of the best ways of capturing and maintaining reader interest. Through dialogue you are passing on information in the most natural way – after all, people communicate through talk – and because the words are those of your characters, you, the author, are hidden.

In the above passage it is quite clear to the experienced reader that although the character doing the talking says that the unknown 'he' has 'got away with it', 'he' has done no such thing; our man on the telephone is certain to go after him. The conflict has been clearly spelled out, and as well as defining the conflict, that snatch of dialogue has also created suspense.

But dialogue is not always the best or most convenient way of hinting at the conflict. Well-written narrative has the advantage of allowing the author to use his descriptive skills outside the constraints of words that issue from the mouth of a character, and must be in character. There is greater freedom, and perhaps more scope for invention, as shown in this extract from my fantasy short story, 'Loop'.

> Six days into his search, north of Amarillo and ten miles out from the shabbiest of those sleepy towns, he pulled the car in close to the rusting red mail box and a mixture of relief and

anticipation washed over him and set his heart thumping as he gazed out at her customized Volkswagen parked at a crazy angle alongside the weather-worn timber stoop.

But what he saw beyond that both confused and appalled him. Nothing fitted in with the restless energy of the girl he'd known intimately for those three days. The sheer neglect and decay confronting him was at odds with her character, and something about it warned him, without subtlety, to turn around and head back through the dry scrub to urban safety.

For some reason this character is searching for a girl. So far the hunt has taken him six days, but now that it seems as if he has found her, he has a premonition of danger.

When summarized in that way, everything seems cloaked in mystery; the narrative passage is hinting at the conflict, not spelling it out. This is typical of the way the nature of a conflict might be gradually revealed in a novel, a bit here, a bit there, until eventually readers have the full picture.

But although very little of the conflict has been revealed, enough seeds have been sown in the minds of readers to make them think, the pace is commendably fast, and I as the author have posed a number of questions which are of a nature serious enough to make readers wonder who, wonder why, and to experience that faint prickle of apprehension that tells them that something – perhaps not very pleasant – is about to happen.

Building Suspense with Scene Reversal

Atmospheric scenes and settings were dealt with in Chapter One but, as you set out on the first chapter of your book, you must be familiar with another vitally important quality that every scene must have if it is to work hard at creating suspense.

I call that quality 'reversal', and the best way of understanding it is to think of the highs and lows you experience in your own life. For example, when you set out to meet someone outside the theatre for your first date together, you feel excited. If they don't turn up, your mood drops through your boots. In the same way, if you set out on that first date convinced that the person you are expecting to meet will not turn up – and they arrive with flowers and a box of chocolates – then your mood will rocket from despondency to euphoria.

In real life, there are scenes that start on highs and end even higher, others that start low and end at rock-bottom. But to create suspense within fictional scenes, that swing between emotional highs and lows must always be present.

When talking about strongly opposing characters, I gave as an example the young man going to his father to ask for a loan to start a business. In a novel, that encounter would be a complete scene, and clearly demonstrates how scene reversal works.

When the the young man enters his father's study to make his request, his hopes will be sky-high, and at the beginning of the scene his father will, perhaps, appear to be willing to listen. But once the request is made he will start to show his opposition to the scheme, and the loan, and there will be a bitter argument. When the young man finally accepts rejection and goes out – slamming the door behind him he is (depending on his character) either in a murderous rage or a deep depression. Either way, the scene reversal is complete.

Because scene reversal is quite obvious to you, the writer, you might argue that it makes each scene predictable, and so destroys the effect; your readers will know that a character's high hopes are going to be dashed, his gloom transformed into joy. But if you think of your own reading, you will know it doesn't work that way. Even knowing what you know now, you will read your next book and begin a scene still hoping that the hero rescues the damsel, or that something will turn up when he fails. Readers read to be entertained, not to analyse how it is done.

When writing your novel you will find yourself following the advice given in Chapter Two, which was to have all your characters disagreeing for most of the time. You will follow it because close study of any published novel will show you that's exactly what happens. In fiction, 'no' is said much more frequently than 'yes'.

Once you have acquired that habit, then in any scenes filled with dialogue, the swing between emotional highs and lows naturally follows. But what you must also do is ensure that scenes with no dialogue follow that same pattern.

When your hero sets out to rescue the heroine, he must successfully fight his way through rugged mountain terrain and raging rapids, only to discover that the heroine has been moved to another location (a swing from high to low). If he sets out on the rescue attempt, knowing it is hopeless, he must be about to turn back in despair when the heroine runs through the woods towards him; she has escaped, and has brought with her the stolen formula (swing from low to high).

In Practice

In this chapter you have seen examples from books that have started with the utmost abruptness ('Gordon Michaels stood in the fountain with all his clothes on'), and from others that have started at a more leisurely pace ('Six days into his search, north of Amarillo and ten miles out from the shabbiest of those sleepy towns, he pulled the car in . . .').

The short, sharp way works for some writers, but if it is not your style you will find that the more leisurely approach will be just as effective provided you put into those first paragraphs the

66

subtle hints that suggest to your readers that something is about to happen. In Chapter One, I used extracts from *The Mary Deare*, by Hammond Innes, and *In Honour Bound* by Gerald Seymour. Both were used to demonstrate setting, but they are also excellent examples of highly effective chapter openings that are less abrupt than some written by Dick Francis.

If adopting this approach means that you cannot put suspense into the first line, you must endeavour to do so very early in your first chapter. Just as scene reversal begins to write itself when your characters are continually in opposition to each other, so this business of starting suspense at the very beginning of your book becomes much easier if you remember to establish the setting and mood and hint at the conflict. While you are doing that, you will also find yourself using foreshadowing, described in detail in the next chapter.

6 Creating Suspense Through Foreshadowing

It has been said about the short story that, because of its brevity, nothing should be written that does not either impart vital information or move the story forwards – preferably both!

The novel is nowhere near so brief, yet if suspense is to be maintained the advice given to short-story writers is just as valid. You should try to give to everything that happens in your novel a meaning. The meaning need not be obvious – indeed, in many cases, and if you are being particularly clever, the meaning will not become clear until readers are nearing the end of the book when they suddenly strike their foreheads with their hands and say, 'Ah, so *that's* what that was all about!'

The particular technique that brings about that reaction is called foreshadowing, and in this chapter we will see:

- How to use immediate foreshadowing
- The impact of obvious foreshadowing
- Foreshadowing through dialogue
- General foreshadowing

How to Use Immediate Foreshadowing

Although foreshadowing is generally taken to mean the technique of dropping subtle hints to readers about what will happen much later in a book, with immediate foreshadowing the effects are felt much sooner.

Immediate foreshadowing is your way of increasing the suspense in a scene by letting readers know, through your prose, that something is going to happen. You can liken it to the way cinema and television directors change the mood of the background music to alert viewers to the silent and unseen approach of the villain. That technique is now so familiar that audiences react with a similar conditioned reflex to that which caused Pavlov's dog to salivate, but as writers we must be much more skilful with our prose.

If you are some way into a thriller your readers will already know that your hero is threatened by villains. But those villains cannot be everywhere, and so there will be periods where your readers become lulled by the lack of menace. Most of the moves your hero makes during such periods will be quite ordinary: eating meals, talking to other people, driving somewhere, turning the key in his own front door and entering his own house.

It is then that you can use immediate foreshadowing. Through the intensity of your prose you change the background music, and suddenly your readers are snapped out of their torpor and feel a quickening of the pulse. In *Tinker, Tailor, Soldier, Spy*, by John le Carré, George Smiley has already checked the Banham deadlock and the Chubb pipe-key securing the front door of his house in King's Road, and the two oak splinters he uses to detect intruders are reassuringly in place when he opens the door and steps into the hall. So the music playing in reader's minds remains placid until Smiley looks about him – and suddenly it changes.

> He was still pondering the question when his gaze fell upon an unfamiliar umbrella in the stand, a silk one with a stitched leather handle and a gold ring with no initial. And it passed

through his mind with a speed which has no place in time that since the umbrella was dry it must have arrived there before six-fifteen when the rain began, for there was no moisture in the stand, either. Also, that it was an elegant umbrella and the ferrule was barely scratched, though it was not new. And that therefore the umbrella belonged to someone agile – even young.

© le Carré Productions 1974. Extract from *Tinker, Tailor, Soldier, Spy* by John le Carré. Reproduced by permission of Hodder and Stoughton Ltd.

The background music analogy is not inappropriate, for any one or all of the senses can be used in immediate foreshadowing. An elderly colonel might enter his darkened country mansion and hear the creak of a floorboard and someone softly and tunelessly whistling upstairs. The lingering smell of cigarette smoke, or of cheap, unfamiliar aftershave, greets a frail old lady as she enters her flat. The hero of your book yawns, gets up from his chair, and as he touches the handle of his bedroom door he feels stickiness and finds congealed blood on his hand. . . .

Imagination is the key. If you have placed a villain in a dark wood and sent your hero walking past, think of those signs that will warn him that something is not quite right: the sudden, startled screech of an owl; a shadow cast by the headlights of a passing car that could not possibly be a tree; the snap of a twig; or the rustle of the bushes on a night when there is no wind.

The Impact of Obvious Foreshadowing

Most foreshadowing is subtle, and this corresponds with the advice given to writers that they should, at all costs, avoid intruding with their own voice. Yet obvious foreshadowing does just that: the writer quite blatantly tells readers about an event that will occur later in the book.

> He signed his name with a flourish, unaware that with a few swift strokes of a fountain pen he had signed away not only his business, but his life.

The writer has intruded shamelessly, for no character in the book could have made that comment. By the use of obvious fore-shadowing, questions have been raised that will inevitably create suspense. The man who has signed his name will die – but why, how, and when?

Here is another example:

> For want of a nail, the kingdom was lost – that's how the catechism goes when you boil it down. In the end you can boil *everything* down to something similar – or so Roberta Anderson thought much later on. It's either all an accident . . . or all fate. Anderson literally stumbled over her destiny in the small town of Haven, Maine, on June 21st, 1988. That stumble was the root of the matter; all the rest was nothing but history.

© Stephen King 1988. Extract from *The Tommyknockers* by Stephen King. Reproduced by permission of Hodder and Stoughton Ltd.

This time the opening passage of the first chapter of *The Tommyknockers*.

There's something else in that book relevant to what we are discussing – what might be called the most obvious of obvious foreshadowing, and a technique used to great effect by early writers of thrillers. It uses obvious foreshadowing as immediate foreshadowing to tickle readers' taste buds at the beginning of a chapter, and is of course the use of chapter headings. 'Anderson

Digs' leads into Chapter Two of *The Tommyknockers*, 'Gardener Takes a Fall' leads into Chapter Five, and 'Tommyknockers, Knocking on the Door' introduces the final chapter.

Exactly the same technique was used in the 1920s by the many unnamed writers of 'Sexton Blake' adventures, and a copy I have in front of me now has chapters with such intriguing headings as: 'Who is Mr. Godfrey Jarrow?'; 'An Amazing Discovery'; and 'Unforseen Disaster'.

Each one of these brief pieces of obvious/immediate foreshadowing creates expectancy (and suspense) in the reader by offering an insight into what is going to happen in the chapter without giving details – and the only way of finding out the full story is by reading on.

Foreshadowing Through Dialogue

Dialogue means people, and people make novels interesting. Foreshadowing occurs naturally in dialogue, and so it is perhaps the easiest and most effective way of creating suspense by this method.

When characters speak, they are thinking aloud. The advice given to all novice writers was quoted at the beginning of this chapter, and if what was suggested becomes second nature to writers then they will always be passing on information, and a lot of that information will come through the mouths of their characters. For a story to advance, most of that information will be about what is going to happen, or the expression of fears about what might happen: in other words, foreshadowing.

'How long was Max put away for?'
    'Three years – but word is he gets out next week, and then there ain't nobody gonna be safe.'

That simple piece of foreshadowing can be manipulated to suit any genre, and shows clearly how effective even a short piece of dialogue foreshadowing can be. For a romantic novel it could be changed to:

'Darling, I hear Clarissa's our new fashion editor.'

'That's right. She takes over next week, my sweet – and God help us all!'

While the writer of horror novels would probably concoct something like:

'Pete, we've locked the cellar door, and the only window has thick iron bars cemented into the brick – but we still can't be sure that'll keep them in, can we?'

'No,' Pete said, and his face was grim. 'Because what we're dealing with is something unknown, something totally alien, and the only thing we know for sure is that if they do get out, every last one of us will die a horrible death.'

I've already suggested that foreshadowing comes naturally to dialogue, and if you have already written quite a lot of fiction those three passages will have been familiar. It's a technique akin to the first part of this familiar advice given to writers of articles: 'Tell them what you're going to tell them; then tell them; then tell them what you've told them.' If you bear that advice constantly in mind – but disregard the third bit unless you are writing a detective story, or adding an epilogue – you will find foreshadowing through dialogue easy, and a sure way of building suspense.

General Foreshadowing

I read somewhere that foreshadowing should be stopped when you are approximately two-thirds of the way through your novel, and that seems to me to be good advice. You must stop some-where; the very nature of foreshadowing tells you that it cannot be continued to the end of the book; and because the last third of any book is usually beginning the taut build-up to the climax, you need to be concentrating on that rather than dropping what will now be pointless hints.

Foreshadowing takes as many forms as your imagination can dream up for dropping suggestive, suspenseful hints to your readers.

Character Traits

The way a character behaves will give a clue to future actions. If a mother tells a child not to go near a dangerous quarry and accepts his obedience when the readers have been told that the child is a liar, they will know what to expect. That technique can be extended to adults, with the story of a yachtsman who has been warned about the treacherous tides by coastguards and has agreed not to venture out of harbour. That is, until one particu-larly stormy day when he is restless and, somewhere beyond the wild waves, a yellow light glimmers. . . .

Missed Signals

Seeing something that does not register can create the first stir-rings of fear in readers. Your hero might walk past a neighbour's leafy suburban driveway at midnight and see a light in one of the eight curtained bedrooms. Preoccupied with his own troubles, he thinks no more about it and the days pass – yet the readers know that the wealthy neighbour is in Spain on business, and will not be back for a month. . . .

Direct Statement of Intent

In dialogue or in introspection, your characters can say exactly what they are going to do without actually specifying a time and place. This happened in real life when one of the two boys involved in the 1987 Jersey murders of Nick and Elizabeth Newall said to his mother, 'One day I'll kill you!'

In Britain, so they say, if we see a wealthy man drive by in a Mercedes the reaction is, 'Why should he have that when I can't afford it?' In America, or so we are told, the response is, 'One day I'll own one of those.' That is another example of foreshadowing by direct statement.

Characters' Actions

By foreshadowing through your characters' actions rather than through thoughts or dialogue, you are painting an immediate, vivid picture.

It can be something as static as a man hidden in the trees watching a young, attractive woman walk through the park, following her with his cold, expressionless eyes from the moment she appears around the curve of the lake until she walks out through the gates.

Or it can be as active and as clearly stated as a youth in a flak jacket at the back of the crowd watching a presidential parade who mimes the actions of pulling the pin and tossing a grenade, his face suffused with hatred and anticipated triumph.

In Practice

Those writers who create their books from a basic idea and dream up the stories as they write will now leap on me and say, if *they* don't know what's going to happen, how can they drop hints to their readers? My answer is that a great deal of – if not all – foreshadowing is done not as you write, but as you rewrite. Even writers who work from an outline are not absolutely certain how a book will turn out. Interesting developments occur to them as they write, making foreshadowing of that particular event impossible – although less impossible if they are using a computer. But even if you do have the convenience of a computer that allows you to scroll back to a convenient point and add your foreshadowing while it is fresh in your mind, you will still find that your best foreshadowing will be done when the first draft is complete and you can view the novel as a whole.

But my earlier point is still valid: stop foreshadowing when you are approximately two-thirds of the way through the book, and get on with the run-up to the climax. Clever readers may be able to work out what is going to happen at the end from the story that has unfolded before them, but the last thing you want to do (except in a traditional detective novel) is to drop hints to make their task easier.

Throughout this chapter it has been clear that when someone asks us what a book is about we can run through plots and subplots and conflicts and crises until we're blue in the face and still not state the obvious: if books are about anything, they are about characters.

So now is the time to look more closely at that one element without which no book can succeed (well, after suspense, that is!).

7 Suspense and Heroes

This chapter – which should be looked upon as a prelude to the one on creating suspense through characters – is a short one, but possibly the most important chapter in this little book.

There are novels that rely on outstanding characters, and others in which the interest is generated through plot. Between those two broad types you have many others that lean one way or the other and so fall somewhere between two stools.

Books with cardboard characters can succeed. But they succeed despite, not because of, those cardboard characters.

If *you* want to succeed, then you must always do your best to make your leading character memorable, and if possible heroic, because only then will readers be concerned enough to care. Only when they care about what is happening – or what is about to happen – to your main character can they enter that now-familiar state we call suspense.

A hero would seem to be a character more usually associated with a thriller or adventure story, and some writers reading this will be grappling with a tender romance (in their novels, that is). But there are all kinds of heroes associated with all walks of life, so stepping outside the limitations of genre let's see if we can work out some basic, defining requisites.

- A hero must have extraordinary courage.
- A hero must be up against an adversary powerful enough to bring out those heroic qualities.

And, believe it or not, that's all that's needed!

The items listed certainly fit in with our notion of an all-action hero from a stirring adventure story. But if you look at those two requisites you will see that the only personal quality needed for heroism is courage and courage comes in many different forms. Physical strength is not needed, because fragile old ladies can be heroic. Intelligence is not needed, either, for courage does not spring from the intellect. Given that courage, then, your hero can be any person, anywhere, in any situation.

It will also be clear that, even given courage, a person could go through a very long life without appearing at all heroic unless he or she is in the right place, at the right time. Something so extraordinary must happen – for an adversary can be a violent storm or a serious illness as well as a human foe – that it can only be tackled by someone with unusual stores of the right kind of courage. The outcome will be that a perfectly ordinary character becomes a hero. (But remember that a hero within the family circle is just as heroic as a hero on the grand scale.)

Put in a slightly different way, the leading characters of your novels will be admired for the courageous way they face up to life's challenges, and the more severe those challenges, the greater the admiration.

But that admiration will also be tinged with disbelief. How long can they go on? How much more can they take? When will it all get too much with them and, inevitably, result in defeat? Through the expoits of a heroic individual, you have created suspense.

Those two requisites mentioned above that together produce a hero at once free you from the restrictions of the adventure story/thriller genres. All you need to do now is put the word 'COURAGE' on one side of a piece of paper, and down the other side list all those extraordinary incidents that can occur within the bounds of your chosen genre.

By doing this you will have created a hero who will be at home in *your* novel. Although the challenges faced may not be as dire as those confronting Indiana Jones in 'The Temple of Doom', they will be believable challenges which readers can identify with, and experience, vicariously, through your truly heroic character.

In Practice

The qualities of courage are all around you, in both real life and fiction. Your own near and extended family and the families of people you know will give you many examples that can be used without change, or with the right amount of exaggeration to make them fit the story you are writing.

But one of the most rewarding and apposite ways of studying heroism as it applies to fiction is to look at fictional heroes. Was Ian Fleming's James Bond a hero? What about Modesty Blaise, and Willie Garvin, Peter O'Donnell's deadly duo? Shane, Jack Schaeffer's eponymous hero, came along to save a Western family, then rode off into the sunset. Taking a step backwards in time, you can look at Alan Quartermain's courage against over-whelming odds in *King Solomon's Mines*, or *She*, by H. Rider Haggard, or study Richard Hannay's exploits in John Buchan's *The Thirty-nine Steps*.

As a close to this chapter, I'd like to point to two very different methods used to portray heroism. The leading characters in Dick Francis's thrillers are all heroes, and the methods this popular writer uses to ensure that his characters are recognized as such make interesting reading. In nearly all cases, the need for a heroic deed comes out of the blue. It is then kept very quiet by the hero until, some time after the event, he is suddenly confronted with it by friends, relatives or acquaintances who have heard the story from an independent source and are awe-struck, astonished, disbelieving or horrified. Throughout, the reluctant hero is suitably modest.

A different method is used by Peter O'Donnell to present Modesty Blaise to enthralled readers. Modesty is given a detailed background that shows her fighting her way up from poverty and degradation to become the boss of a violent outfit based somewhere in the Mediterranean region. When she leaves that group to go solo with her assistant, Willie Garvin – invariably rescuing one or more people from the clutches of superhuman villains – we watch her perform her feats in front of everybody, 'goodies' and villains. Rather than being reflected, Modesty Blaise's heroism is immediate.

8   Creating Suspense Through Characters

In this chapter we will be looking at characters for themselves, at what makes them tick, at the way they speak and act, at the way they add to a novel's suspense in a way that is separate from the techniques we have discussed earlier in this book.

We will be looking at how to:

- Create expectancy through predictable character reactions
- Shock with unpredictable character reactions
- Heighten the suspense with crisp, sparkling dialogue
- Reveal your characters gradually
- Use intelligent introspection

Create Expectancy Through Predictable Character Reactions

The creation of living, breathing characters with all the strengths and foibles that makes each one an individual is at the root of this method of putting suspense into your novel. Sound advice given to budding novelists is always to write a brief description of each character on an index card and keep it close to hand at each writing session. That résumé will include a dominant character trait, and to establish each character firmly in the minds of your readers you will reveal that outstanding distinguishing feature quite soon after each one has made an appearance.

How you do this will vary. A curmudgeonly old colonel will bluster and puff and fume; you will give him the vocabulary and the manner to suit. A hothead – man or woman – with a tendency towards violence will be shown flying off the handle and perhaps lashing out with fists or feet. Someone with a soft heart will weep at the drop of a hat, while the cold, unemotional sort will walk past the bleeding bodies at a terrible traffic accident without turning a hair or offering to help.

You will come up with your own cast of characters neatly tailored to fit into the type of book you are writing. But one of the important things to remember while you are imbuing your characters with distinctive mannerisms and behavioural quirks is that when you pack your book with people who act with complete predictability – in total accord with that dominant character trait – you have at once provided yourself with an invaluable suspense tool.

The most obvious example to use as an illustration is 'Hothead'. Your readers will know what to expect of this character, and will be either trembling or licking their lips in anticipation: given the right provocation, there will be a violent explosion.

We must now look back to Chapter Two, in which the fourth section was devoted to the creation of strongly opposing characters. What you do next is bring into your cast of characters a man who always speaks his mind (and has the broken nose to show for it). Your plot has been carefully contrived to give these two characters (Loud Mouth and Hothead) entirely contrary views about whatever conflict you have devised. Finally, all you need to do is put both of them in the same room at the same time – and you have created a situation fraught with suspense.

Your readers *know* that Loud Mouth is going to say something to upset Hothead, and they know that when he does he is going to get a black eye to go with the crooked nose. The only things they don't know are when the inflammatory words are going to be uttered, and how long after that before the explosion.

Shock with Unpredictable Character Reactions

But what if there is no explosion?

Once you have decided that a character will be a lion, or a mouse, you will then proceed to demonstrate this characteristic to your readers, scene by scene. In other words, although you may have used direct exposition to tell your readers that this man is a lion, you need to plant the image of a lion firmly in their minds through your character's own actions.

As we have already seen, this process gives you superb opportunities to raise the suspense within a scene. However, once the character's dominant trait becomes firmly established, the suspense then reaches further.

If he explodes into violent rage within one scene, the expectancy is that he will do it again and again as the book progresses. In your plot you will sometimes deliberately let your readers see the way ahead, at other times subtly hint at what might happen through foreshadowing which, for knowledgeable readers, is often just as illuminating. Either way, their tense feelings of anticipation will now be connected to events much further ahead in the book. The suspense created through predictable character reactions is working well.

But now you pull the rug, and in so doing tighten the strings of the big bull fiddle called suspense close to breaking-point. You cause your oh-so-predictable character to react in a completely *unpredictable* way, but you are careful to do it so that, on reflection and with the benefit of hindsight, it was entirely *predictable*.

And if that sounds like utter gibberish, let me explain.

In life, you have an uncle who for as long as you have known him has been miserable and bad-tempered. He is always nasty. As a child, you visited your aunt on Sunday afternoons and if you disturbed your uncle's after-dinner snooze he bit your head off. When you were a young mother he complained that your children were bad-mannered and noisy.

If that man were to change, overnight and without warning, it would be unbelievable. Your fictional characters must, in some important respects, behave as real-life characters, so, if we are going to make one of them act contrary to their dominant character trait, we must give warning. We must devise an incident, or a series of incidents, with a cumulative effect, that might possibly nudge our predictable character off his unswerving path through life.

I deliberately used the words 'possibly', and 'nudge'. That's because, for maximum effect, we must again be rather subtle. An incident that shocks our character so that he is definitely blown off that straight line defeats the object. The future act that is meant to be unexpected would again become predictable, and we would be back where we started.

Let's take our violent Mr Hothead.

Supposing his mother burnt her hand on the gas stove one Saturday evening while baking, and he had to drive her to casualty. And suppose, while there (this is a busy city hospital), our Hothead sees a constant stream of injured people arriving, many of them the victims of muggings or brawls outside pubs. Perhaps one of the drunken youths attacks a young nurse, and she is badly shaken. Perhaps, at one point, somebody becomes so violent that he finds himself actually helping to restrain the offender.

We need to be circumspect, and the purpose of this particular scene (to explain future unpredictable behaviour) has already been partially masked by what caused it (the mother's injury). We can camouflage it still further by bringing another of our characters on stage at casualty and having him/her involved in a conversation with Hothead that further advances the plot, and serves further to distract the reader from our nefarious bamboozlement.

The seed has been planted (in another example of foreshadowing – negative foreshadowing? Preparing readers for something that isn't going to happen). The next time our Hothead gets the urge to thump somebody on the nose he will get a quick flash of the interior of casualty, and hold back. Nothing will be said. It's not even necessary to slip inside his mind and show his thinking. It's enough that he has turned the other cheek, and the readers will immediately know the reason.

And, of course, we've now gleefully created total confusion. From now on, readers won't know *what* to expect from Hothead. Is he a reformed character? Or, once the images of those broken and bleeding bodies in casualty fade, will he return to his violent ways?

Heighten the Suspense with Crisp, Sparkling Dialogue

Dialogue is what draws people to television soap operas. Since the 1950s, *Coronation Street* has kept people in suspense through the words put into the mouths of characters by skilled writers. *Cheers* kept people laughing for a decade by the same means.

Although the lines were not exactly literature, I would suggest that in the quotations in the earlier chapter on foreshadowing the dialogue was, if not the most effective part, then certainly the part that caught your eye. Nowadays, a book without a lot of good dialogue simply won't work.

Listen to this:

'Dr Paige Taylor.' The district attorney's voice was filled with disgust. He turned to Gus Venable, his chief prosecuting attorney. 'I'm handing this trial over to you, Gus. I want a conviction. Murder One. The gas chamber.'

'Don't worry,'Gus Venable said quietly. 'I'll see to it.'

© Sidney Sheldon 1994. Extract from *Nothing Lasts Forever* by Sidney Sheldon. Reproduced by permission of HarperCollins Publishers Ltd.

Now here's something completely different.

He has his mother's beauty and his father's body: a swan's head atop a pit bull. When he embraces Sally, she smells turps and a whiff of garlic on his straggly blonde moustache.

'Spaghetti again?' she asks. 'Al olio?'

'Again,' he says with his quirky smile.

'I can't complain, we had fettuccini. Ma sends her love. Pa doesn't send his.'

Eddie nods. 'How is the old man?'

'Terrible. Smoking and drinking up a storm. I don't know why he's paying that fancy Park Avenue doc. He never does what he's told.'

'He still got that girl in Brooklyn?'

'Oh, sure. I can't blame him for that, can you?'

' Yes,' Eddie Steiner says, 'I can blame him.'

© Lawrence Sanders 1988. Extract from *Timothy's Game* by Lawrence Sanders. Reproduced by permission of Hodder and Stoughton Ltd.

The first of these pieces has been selected because it is terse, modern writing – written in the third person – that manages to say and do an awful lot in just four lines. Let's examine what has been achieved. We now know two people's occupations, and we know a little of their customary manner from their mode of speech. It's also clear that the district attorney is unlikely to show mercy to criminals, and because the DA is putting his faith in his chief prosecuting attorney, that man must be clinically efficient, and highly successful.

This is also, incidentally, an excellent example of the creation of suspense by foreshadowing through dialogue; readers have been told what the book is about, and will now be desperate to find out if this young woman, Paige Taylor, is found guilty and sent to her death.

Lawrence Sanders writes the Timothy Cone books in the first person, and although that style might appear to be distracting, you get used to it after one page and after two you're beginning to wonder why you read anything else. This quotation is longer, the writing more idiosyncratic. The choice of the present tense gives the writing immediacy, and it is full of foreshadowing and innuendo, and tells readers something about both characters involved.

Sally is tolerant, Eddie is the reverse: they have opposite views on their father's philandering. But they are both concerned about his smoking and drinking, and because Sally mentions in what is almost a humorous aside that he is ignoring doctor's orders, we know he is going to die (foreshadowing). Ma sends her love, Pa doesn't send his, so we know that Eddie is doing something that his mother can accept but his father bitterly opposes (Eddie is gay).

The next extract is shown not for what it says, but for the wonderfully skilful way it is said. It's taken from John le Carré's *Our Game,* and is a marvellous example of crisp dialogue that wastes not a single syllable and proceeds at tremendous pace.

Instead of answering, Luck addressed himself to me. 'Which languages does Pettifer speak, precisely, apart from Russian?'

'Precisely, I don't know.' He didn't like that. 'He's a Slavonic scholar. Languages are his forte, minority languages particularly. I had the impression he picked them up as he went along. He's something of a philologist too, I believe.'

'In his blood, is it?'

'Not to my knowledge. He has the flair.'

'Like you, then?'

'I have application.'

'And Pettifer hasn't?' ·

'He doesn't need it. I told you, he has flair,'

'When did he last travel abroad, to your knowledge?'

'Travel? Good heavens, he travelled all the time. Used to. It was his passion. The more unsavoury a place, the better he liked it.'

© 1995 by David Cornwell. Extract from *Our Game* by John le Carré. Reproduced by permission of Random House, Inc.

Reveal Your Characters Gradually

This is the technique delightfully but aptly referred to as peeling the onion skin. It also demonstrates clearly that there are varying degrees of suspense.

Waiting to see if the stem is going to break when your hero is dangling over a fifty-foot cliff with nothing more substantial to hold on to than a tender cowslip is nerve-racking suspense. He survives, and you discover that at the moment of crisis he was feeling sorry for the gallant little primula. The reason behind that sensitivity – and much more besides – is gradually revealed to you over several chapters. This is the revelation of character, and suspense of a much gentler kind.

There are a number of ways to reveal the many facets of character, and because you should take time peeling the onion skin you should also make it the opportunity to flex your ingenuity. They include:

- Direct statement by you (*He was a hard man, Joe Bloggs*)
- The character's own revealing dialogue (*'Get out. Now. Before I throw you out!'*)
- The character's actions (*He is seen physically throwing somebody out*)
- Other people's dialogue (*'Did you see that? He opened the door, picked him up by the seat of the pants and the scruff of the neck and threw him bodily down the steps!'*)
- Introspection or interior monologue (*All right, so Kong was tough. But after ten years battling terrorists with the SAS and eight more married to a woman who could bend iron bars between her teeth, Cecil knew he could throw him out without raising a sweat*)

That last example is a pointer to where you should begin your onion peeling, and how not to do it: you should start with your character's name, but no hard man in your book should ever be called Cecil Smith, no shrinking violet given a name like Rocky Graziano (a real-life middleweight boxer from days gone by, and thus a superb role-model).

I have already said that this is suspense of the gentle kind, and you will find in novels by such authors as Joanna Trollope that characters are still revealing something about themselves when the book reaches its conclusion. Indeed, just as the denouement is the satisfying climax at which all problems are solved and all loose ends neatly tied, so you can make it the moment when the last piece of the fascinating jigsaw that is your protagonist's character drops neatly into place. If you can achieve that, then you will know that at least some of your carefully cultivated suspense has been maintained to the very end.

In the brief examples of methods of revealing character that I gave above, the actual detail disclosed was that the man was tough. But your readers will want to know how and why he became that way, and so in addition to the index card that you keep by you as you write you will need, in a separate file, a full, written description of your characters from the time they were born. This will show every aspect of their development, and will enable readers to judge for themselves which characteristics are inherited, and which have been shaped by life.

But do remember that we are always thinking in terms of suspense, and peeling the onion skin. We have already seen how our good friend Hothead thumping somebody on the nose can contribute to suspense through predictable and unpredictable character reactions. But now we are dealing with prolonged suspense through the slow unveiling of character, and in order to achieve that in such a situation you must ensure that a couple of your minor characters are there to speculate on the deep-seated reasons for his striking the blow.

One of them might believe that his violence comes from his drunken father – either inherited, or by example. The other will disagree, and say it was because of his time spent in the commandos. If there's a third, he might believe Hothead simply enjoys what he's doing (but that, too, will have some deep-rooted cause). Through those speculations by other characters in your novel you have given your readers something to think about. They might disagree with all those theories, and have one or more of their own. If they do, so much the better, for the purpose of suspense is to make readers turn pages.

Incidentally, for the purpose of credibility, your minor characters will need to be on stage, and speculating, for a legitimate reason. In this case they could be the policemen and women who break up the fracas; the doctors who repair the broken bones or stitch the gashes; or friends who know Hothead, though not well enough to explain his actions.

Use Intelligent Introspection

We have already looked briefly at introspection as one of the techniques a writer can use to reveal details of character. But your main character will be thinking all the way through your novel, and the intelligent use and clever disclosure of innermost thoughts is one of the finest ways of creating suspense.

If you have done your job well, your readers will know and love – or at least empathize with – your main character; if you are writing in the first person that identification will be very strong. Readers will be anxious to learn more about him and, in order to keep them in suspense, you will be carefully stripping away those onion skins and revealing details a smidgen at a time. When you allow your readers free access to your main character's thoughts, the opportunities for planting the seeds of suspense are suddenly unlimited.

- Readers can listen to your character worrying and expressing fears that would never be spoken aloud in conversation.
- They can listen to speculation about what the character imagines or predicts might happen later in the book; wild flights of fancy about unlikely developments that seem preposterous – yet just might be true.
- When writing in the first person, or third person impersonal, and able to enter into the thoughts of just the one character, the writer is able to make readers privy to that character's feelings, opinions and speculation about other characters – a valuable tool.

- When writing in the multiple third person, readers can follow the main character's thoughts when decisions are being made. Suspense can be high if readers have previously been inside *other* character's thoughts, and know the decision being made by the main character is a potentially fatal mistake.

Many authors find introspection quite easy to write. Although there must always be adherence to the principle of advancing the story at all times, the very nature of thought makes it necessary for some pleasant rambling to take place. And if you have been avidly absorbing the many suspense techniques expounded so far, you will realize that some relaxed thinking on the part of your main character is just the thing you need to lull your readers into a false sense of security before hitting them with an almighty bang.

In other words, let your main character lapse into some benign mental ambling that seems to be leading nowhere – then have him make that sudden, unexpected and flawed decision that not only creates suspense, but leaves readers somewhat shell-shocked.

Warren didn't want to get caught out here on a small craft some thirty miles from shore in case any storm was on the way. Not much traffic out here, just your occasional fishing boat and now and then a big motor cruiser passing by in the distance. But the way he figured it, all of these boat people knew more about weather than he did, so as long as there was *anybody* out here, he didn't feel foolhardy. Minute he saw any boats heading in, he'd be right behind them. Meanwhile, if there was any danger he expected he'd begin hearing Coast Guard advisories on the weather channels.

© Hui Corporation 1966. Extract from *Gladly the Cross-Eyed Bear* by Ed McBain. Reproduced by permission of Hodder and Stoughton Ltd.

The passage above is a typical example of introspection that just might be erroneous thinking. It shows a nervous man who knows nothing about boats relying for his safety on others he *believes* are knowledgeable, and on the *expectation* of hearing Coast Guard warnings.

This final extract is a straightforward example of melodramatic introspection designed to raise suspense, and is extremely effective.

Victor's heart was racing and he felt an unpleasant sensation in his abdomen. 'Please make the baby normal,' he prayed to himself. He looked over at his wife as his eyes clouded with tears. She had wanted another baby so much. He felt himself begin to tremble again. He chided himself inwardly. 'I shouldn't have done it. But please, God – let this baby be all right.' He looked up at the clock. The second hand seemed to drag slowly around the face. He wondered how much longer he could stand the tension.

© Robin Cook 1989. Extract from *Mutation* by Robin Cook. Macmillan, 1989.

In Practice

Although characters should not be taken straight from real life, you will invariably create your characters by blending characteristics and visual features from people you know, or have seen – even from memorable characters you have enjoyed watching or reading about in films and books.

From careful study of such material you will see examples of predictable and unpredictable character reactions, and sparkling dialogue. By looking closer to home, you will gain valuable insights into intelligent introspection (simply listen to your own thought processes) and the way character can be revealed by peeling the onion skin.

For this you will need to look at friends or relatives whose life-history you know intimately. Select one person, and write their life story down chronologically. Then study what you have got – birthplace, schooling, profession, military service – highlight important stages or events, and see how each of those could be revealed to great effect at different times in a work of fiction.

This is one of the ways some writers work: they create detailed life stories for each of their leading characters, and use selected highlights from that story to bring their character to life; gradually, step by step, always holding something back so that their readers, like yours, will always be in suspense.

9 Creating Suspense Through Viewpoint

This strange process of creating suspense becomes more and more interesting with each chapter – even (or perhaps especially) for me, and I'm writing this book! By interesting I mean that as I work my way through, raising each topic and explaining and illustrating each point, it becomes increasingly obvious that suspense really is the most important element of any novel.

Now that, of course, is a personal opinion. But if one argument against it is that plot is more important, then the reply is that one of the main purposes of any plot is to create suspense. If another argument is that all books must start with character, then I'll agree – but that character must be doing something, and what he is doing (because its unforseen outcome is in the future) inevitably leads to suspense.

What I am getting around to in a convoluted sort of way is that while it might seem that the choice of viewpoint is not necessarily determined by its effect on the creation of suspense, on closer examination it certainly is.

Because of that I am going to look at viewpoint from just two angles: single-person viewpoint, and multi-person viewpoint (variously known as multiple, God's eye, omniscient, and third person impersonal; throughout this book I will use the latter term).

The subjects to be covered are:

- Suspense through single-person viewpoint (first and third)

- Increasing suspense opportunities using third person impersonal
- Switching viewpoint for maximum suspense

Suspense Through Single-person Viewpoint (First and Third)

First Person

When we write letters, we use the pronoun 'I'. Not only is this a method of writing with which we are familiar, it is an excellent way of making the people reading our letters feel as if we are actually talking to them. It is personal, cosy, even intimate.

If it achieves those effects when we write letters, it will do the same when we write a novel. If our narrator is Dick Turpin, as soon as we begin writing the readers will hear Dick Turpin's voice talking. They will feel as if he is telling the story exclusively to them, revealing only to them his secrets, his innermost thoughts. Because readers are so close to the 'I' of the book it seems, in a way, as if everything is revealed through the intimacy of introspection.

This intimacy with the book's main character – this feeling of actually *being* the main character – has an enormous bonus for the writer keen to create suspense: readers are living the book, so everything that happens (to the main character) is happening to them. They are involved. They feel the pain and the laughter, the grief and the excitement – and the pulsating anxiety when, by one of the methods we have discussed, you have hinted that something is about to go terribly wrong.

You have already seen one brilliant example of first-person viewpoint, and it's well worth repeating here in its original form, and then slightly modified, to illustrate a remarkable difference in effect.

Here again, in first-person viewpoint, is the extract from *Straight*, by Dick Francis:

I inherited my brother's life. Inherited his desk, his business, his gadgets, his enemies, his horses and his mistress. I inherited my brother's life, and it nearly killed me.

© Dick Francis 1989. Extract from *Straight* (Michael Joseph, 1989). Reproduced by permission of Penguin Books Ltd.

Now here it is once more, but this time in third-person viewpoint:

He inherited his brother's life. Inherited his desk, his business, his gadgets, his enemies, his horses and his mistress. He inherited his brother's life, and it nearly killed him.

If you read both those passages very slowly in an effort to get the maximum effect from the words, you will notice a startling difference. The first is highly personal; you are involved; the person who was nearly killed is you. Reading through the second one after you have read the first (and I must admit that is cheating a bit, tending to over-emphasize the difference) there is a feeling almost of detachment, of couldn't-care-less. Certainly you would lose that uninterested feeling as the book progressed and you began to learn more about this mysterious 'he', but you would never experience the dramatic, hammer-blow effect of that passage written in the first person and detailing, in just three lines, the problems (and joys!) you are about to face in the next three hundred or so pages.

And that's because the 'I' says you are involved, while the 'he' is involving somebody else.

Third Person

For the purpose of creating suspense, single third-person viewpoint is almost identical to first-person viewpoint, and because this book is studying viewpoint for that purpose alone, I am not going to go into details.

Suffice it to say that although the way I have described first-person viewpoint would seem to make it ideal for our purposes, it has its drawbacks, and if you spend time browsing in your library you will find many more books written in single third person.

It is when you enter the world of third person impersonal or omniscient viewpoint that the suspense possibilities become virtually unlimited.

Increasing Suspense Opportunities Using Third Person Impersonal

The 'don't know' principle

When writing a novel using either of the single-person viewpoints, the big drawback is that everything must be revealed to your readers through your viewpoint character. You cannot suddenly switch viewpoint and step inside other characters to reveal their thoughts, feelings, and plans,

This is not necessarily bad for suspense. Careful foreshadowing in all its forms subtly prepares readers for later dramatic incidents, crisp dialogue and intelligent introspection keeps the story moving forwards and creates anticipation; skilful characterization creates empathy with the main character so that readers become more and more concerned; and in single-person viewpoint the suspense is built up by the principle of 'don't know', rather than 'do know'.

Readers are waiting for something to happen but, except in a vague sense, they don't know the details. When the breathless hero jumps out of his Aston Martin at the railway cutting, finds that the heroine is no longer lashed to the rails awaiting the arrival of the express and realizes he has walked into a trap, it is a profound shock for the readers. But what we are concerned with here is how to create the maximum amount of suspense leading up to those shocks, and the way to do that is to make readers privy to all.

Well, almost all!

The 'do know' principle

Not knowing what is going to happen can be unsettling, and in many circumstances very frightening. For example, a first visit to the dentist will be an experience that is horribly familiar to most people.

But knowing exactly what is going to happen can be even worse. Using the same familiar example, the second visit to the dentist does not bring with it fear of the unknown, but fear of the known. This time you know what is going to happen, you have experienced the needle's sharp prick, you remember the whine and the bite of the drill – and you know the helpless, vertiginous feeling of lying tilted so far back in the chair that coins start tinkling from your pockets.

The difference between those two visits to the dentist is the difference that can be created in your story through the use of the third person impersonal.

Readers are following the trials and tribulations of someone with toothache. Through first person viewpoint they will stay with that person in the waiting room. By means of multi-person viewpoint they can be with the patient, experiencing all his worries and fears. They can then leave him and step inside the surgery to watch the dentist preparing his needles and drills, listen to him telling his assistant exactly what he is going to do to the terrified patient in the other room.

Switching Viewpoint for Maximum Suspense

Let's look again at our hero leaping from his Aston Martin to rescue the young woman tied to the railway lines.

If we were writing this in single-person viewpoint our hero would learn what the villains are up to, discover by some means where the young woman is being held, then drive off at high speed hoping to arrive in time to pluck her from the path of the screaming locomotive. When he arrives at the location after a frantic drive through dark, leafy lanes, he finds she has either been moved, or was never there. Suddenly, a pistol cracks from the nearby woods, and a bullet whines over his head.

In third person impersonal, it might be done this way:

Hero gets a telephone message telling him that the young woman will be found tied to the railway lines at a certain location. He prepares to rescue her.

Switch viewpoint to the criminals, in a remote farmhouse. A telephone message has been sent, with the young woman listening. She is now securely bound, and locked in the cellar. The villains make their way to the railway line, prepared to shoot the hero when he arrives.

Switch viewpoint to the young woman. She is frantically sawing at her bonds with a piece of broken glass, knowing that if she doesn't escape and warn the hero, he will die.

Switch back to the hero. He is on his way, and nearing the location.

Because we have used third person impersonal, the situation is now fraught with suspense. The readers are one step ahead of the hero. They know the villains' dastardly plans, and they know that if the hero proceeds according to *his* plan, he will probably die.

But they have also been in the dank cellar with the young woman, and watched her struggling to escape. If she succeeds, she can save the hero – but how can she can get to the railway ahead of the villains?

A *Taste for Death* was written by Peter O'Donnell in 1989, and featured his popular duo, Modesty Blaise and Willie Garvin. At one point in the book, criminals lead by a man called Gabriel are trying to locate a blind girl who is being protected by Garvin.

They find where she is being held, and although she manages to escape, Garvin is captured. Now comes the viewpoint switching that you will recognize.

Modesty Blaise is with Sagasta, of the Panama Police. She realizes that Garvin has probably been caught.

Switch viewpoint to Garvin, at a hotel, in the hands of the criminals. After much talk, Gabriel arrives and says he wants a woman called Rosita to come and fix up a parcel for Garvin. After a switch of viewpoint of little significance, readers are brought back to Garvin, where the woman Rosita is preparing a bomb. Gabriel then announces that it is time to make the telephone call to draw Modesty Blaise into a trap.

Switch viewpoint to Modesty Blaise. The telephone call comes, telling her that Garvin will meet her in the hotel lobby at two o'clock. She suspects a trap, but knows she must go.

Switch to Garvin. The trap has been set for Modesty. She will be met in the lobby by a man with a machine-gun. Garvin cannot help. He now has one hand secured to a radiator with a handcuff, the other is stretched out holding the bomb at arm's length. A wire leads from the bomb's detonator through a system of eye-rings and tubes to the door, where it is secured. If Garvin lowers his arm, it will detonate the bomb. If Modesty Blaise gets past the man in the lobby, when she opens the door it will detonate the bomb.

If you examine that segment of plot you will see that it is almost identical to the little scenario with the young woman and the railway line. This method of switching to and from between hero and criminals allows readers to be privy to all. They know exactly what fiendish traps have been set, and with baited breath they watch the hero walk into them.

If it was pantomime, or the Saturday morning picture club,

children would be standing up in their seats shouting, 'Look out, it's a trap!' Readers cannot do that, they must sit and wait. The result? Suspense.

Once again, I appear to have been concentrating on the thriller genre, but this technique of switching viewpoint to create suspense can be used to great effect by writers of all kinds of fiction. The basic principle is that you let readers know what is going to happen while the main character is still in the dark.

This means that you can put a young man called Greg in a taxi with a diamond ring in his pocket and send him to Karen's flat to propose but then you can switch viewpoint to Karen's flat and show her telling her enthralled friend that she has decided to finish the relationship with Greg.

Perhaps one of the best and most accessible ways of studying this technique in action is to watch television soaps. Each short scene is an example of switched viewpoint. In a bewildering sequence of snatched images and conversations the viewers are constantly being let into secrets so that they are always one step ahead of . . . well, of virtually everybody!

And therein lies the warning. This is a technique that can add tremendous suspense to your novels, but it should be used with circumspection. Remember, always, that even when using multi-person viewpoint you should establish reader rapport with your main character. Switch too frequently, leave your readers too long with other characters, and that rapport can be lost.

For suspense to work, your readers must care deeply.

In Practice

A story, or parts of a story, can be told without any viewpoint at all, and I have made that mistake several times. I say mistake simply because, without viewpoint, readers are in a kind of limbo or void, following the actions of a group of characters without being intimately associated with any one of them.

That immediately negates the important statement made above: 'for suspense to work, readers must care deeply.'

Nevertheless, this method of writing might have its uses. You may be writing a prologue, an epilogue, or simply writing a scene that is deliberately intended to be impersonal.

But to maintain suspense these non-viewpoint episodes should be few and far between, and my purpose for bringing them up at all is to point out their limited worth, and the essential difference between viewpoint, and non-viewpoint – for, after all, talking about viewpoint is one thing, understanding it is another.

So, somewhat belatedly, may I say now that unless you enter into a character's thoughts, there is no viewpoint. 'He said' or 'she said,' even 'Frank said' or 'Helen said', mean nothing in terms of viewpoint. But if you say, 'Frank said sharply, and as he looked into her eyes he at once realized that his words were falling on deaf ears', then you have entered Frank's thoughts and immediately created a viewpoint character.

This important point now suggests a rule that is not mandatory, but certainly advisable: when switching viewpoint in third person impersonal either from scene to scene or chapter to chapter – always ensure that you choose one strong viewpoint character.

What this boils down to in practice is that if you are with the 'goodies' in one scene, the leading 'goodie' will be your viewpoint character. The same will apply if, in the next scene, you switch to the 'baddies'. In this way, you personalize the contest between the forces of good and evil – and, once again, your readers care deeply.

10   Overlapping for Suspense

In the previous chapter we saw how switching from one character to another when using the third person impersonal (multi-person viewpoint) heightened the suspense in your story by putting readers one step ahead of the game. By entering the mind of different, carefully selected individuals, your readers could listen to plans and, for example, know that the girl supposedly tied to the railway lines waiting to be killed by the next express train was actually quite safe (well, reasonably so), and our hero was being lured into a trap set by the baddies.

The technique of overlapping (sometimes called linking) is similar. Once again the readers are taken into the writer's confidence, in that they are given advance information that puts them always a step ahead of one character, or one group of characters, at a time. It is the 'do know' principle all over again, but with a very important difference, and it is the technique that we will be studying in this short but important chapter.

Create Suspense Through Overlapping Chapters

As you saw in Chapter Nine, letting your readers know what villains are planning when your poor hero is in ignorance – and the other way round – is a wonderfully cunning way of creating suspense.

In that chapter we did it simply by switching viewpoint. Readers were allowed to watch action, listen to conversation, eavesdrop on people's thoughts. Then, at the opportune moment, there was a cut from one scene/character to another and, armed with privileged information, readers watched with bated breath as this fresh character bowled merrily along to certain disaster. I called this the exploitation of the 'do know' principle, which is much more effective for creating unbearable suspense than the 'don't know' principle, because it's like a second visit to the dentist: readers know exactly what is going to happen.

Overlapping can once again make use of the technique of switching from one character/scene to another when employing multi-person viewpoint. But the important difference I mentioned earlier is related to time. Previously, we switched viewpoint in a straightforward chronological way. With overlapping, we also fiddle with time in the interests of suspense.

Let's take another look again at our hero in the Aston Martin who is racing to save the young lady who, he has been told, is tied to the railway lines.

This time, let's imagine that he got the bad news via his mobile phone. Stranded, without a car, miles from his apartment, he is forced to thumb a lift. He is picked up by two men in a fast car, transported to the desired location in town, and dropped.

Readers now stay with the two men in the car (viewpoint has been switched). They are two of the villains (not too much of a coincidence; the hero was thumbing a lift on their chosen route), and readers stay with them as they drive on to a remote farmhouse where the young lady is being guarded by other villains. There they pick up two more men and various weapons, and drive to the main railway line and prepare the trap.

Now viewpoint is switched again. Back with the hero, at the time we left him and at the place where he was dropped, we go with him as he walks to his flat. There, he telephones the young lady's home, gets no answer, and at once jumps into his car and races to where he has been told she has been placed in peril. He drives straight into the trap.

As you can see from this example, the technique of overlapping is a refinement of simple viewpoint switching. Instead of listening to the villains planning to set a trap then going on to see what the hero will do, we actually stay with the villains and watch them at work. Then we jump back in time. Another switch in viewpoint takes us back to the hero where we left him, and we now stay with him until the resolution of this particular climax.

In the particular example I am using, the difference between viewpoint switching and overlapping is more than just that difference in time. It is the difference between reading a static scene in which villains plan a trap, and reading an action scene in which they drive to the woods overlooking the railway line, choose the positions from where they can catch the hero in a withering crossfire, and then settle down in the darkness, rifles at the ready, to wait for his arrival.

Suspense is now based not on hearsay, but on your readers' clear image of what faces the hero. And as the hero telephones to check that the young lady really is missing, envisages her in her awful predicament and girds his loins preparatory to a daring rescue, what the readers see is the image of the villains crouched in the dark woods waiting to ambush him, and it stays with them to heighten the suspense.

In Practice

A little earlier I talked about overlapping chapters, but the same principles can also be applied to scenes. Breaks in a book come in different degrees. There is the double space within a chapter with the same scene continued unchanged after the break; the same space, followed by a switch in viewpoint; and then the clear, sharp break between chapters.

Whenever you decide that a break should be inserted, either in a scene or a chapter – and one of your main guidelines should be to make that break when the opportunity to create suspense is at its highest – always look at the possibility of overlapping. But do beware. Like any other technique, overdoing it can lessen the effect, so don't get to the stage where you are overlapping every-thing in sight.

You will find from your own experience, and from the exam-ple of our hero in the Aston Martin, that overlapping works best when there is plenty of movement. Indeed, it is difficult to see how overlapping could work without groups of characters moving about in different locations.

I think overlapping is best summarized like this. Readers watch one group of characters going somewhere and doing something that will seriously affect another group of characters. Usually, it is the 'baddies' doing something that will have dire consequences for the 'goodies' The clock is put back, viewpoint is then switched, and from that point in time and from that second viewpoint, the story is continued until the groups come together again and the situation is resolved.

To demonstrate, here is another example:

A number of ragged, heavily armed bandits wend their way on horseback through a mountain pass, descend the other side and make camp, confident that they have not been seen. Switch viewpoint and put the clock back, and a second group is watching them from the high ground as they enter the pass.

If you carefully study published novels, you will discover that you have been reading overlapping scenes and chapters without realizing what was going on. Quite often, a telephone is involved. Readers will be following a scene in which someone is talking on the telephone. The telephone is put down, and the scene continues – often at length. Then there is a break – either a scene break, or chapter break. After the break, the clock is put back, and viewpoint is switched to the person at the other end of the line just as they are replacing the receiver.

When writing your own novels you will find that the two methods of overlapping I have mentioned briefly above will not only be of use to you, but they will suggest many others. And like any of the suspense techniques in this book, the various kinds of overlapping can be taken and adapted so that they will slot neatly into any genre.

11 Creating Suspense Through Readers' Expectations

Nearly every situation in life comes with built-in suspense. I mentioned this in the introduction, describing how each of us goes through life wondering what will happen next. Often suspense is of the 'will they/won't they?' kind. Will George pass his driving test? Will Wayne get his A-levels? Will I have saved enough for my holidays by August? Will my short story/novel sell? Will I ever master the technique of creating suspense in fiction?

Looked at in that way, this book becomes nothing more than an exposition of the technique of exploiting, expanding and intensifying everyday situations, then manipulating them for our specific purpose.

Put that way, too, it becomes the useless kind of gobbledygook I've been trying to avoid, so let's move on.

In this chapter we will be looking at:

- How certain situations create spontaneous suspense
- How to confuse and misinform to create the suspense of uncertainty
- Suspense through the use of Kipling's 'honest serving-men'
- Creating suspense using threats – specific and implied

How Certain Situations Create Spontaneous Suspense

To make it easy for myself I can begin this section by going over old material. For example, the whole of Chapter One is concerned with the use of scenery to create suspense; not strictly *situations*, but certainly suspense of the spontaneous kind.

Much of Chapter Nine was also concerned with spontaneous suspense: impose a time-limit on a situation, and readers automatically start to worry if things are going to get done before it's too late.

But there are many more situations that have built-in suspense, and although each one could possibly be condensed into a short phrase (or the 'will they/won't they' kind), it is useful to look at them in some detail.

Indeed, I suppose that, in a way, this section is offering hints on what to write about.

Puzzles

A good book that presents the reader with a puzzle is intriguing. Because people want to know the answer – and often want to see if they can work it out for themselves before the author divulges all – they will keep reading.

If you begin turning the pages of Robert Harris's *Enigma*, you will experience instant suspense. The 'Enigma' of the title is a German code system used during the Second World War, so the book is about one of the purest forms of puzzle. As I write this I am exactly halfway through that marvellous book, and I can vouch for its page-turning qualities.

Agatha Christie used puzzles, as did and do all the other writers of traditional detective fiction, and if, sometimes, the characterization suffers a little from the concentration on plot, few readers are concerned.

Impossible Goals

This is the legendary 'Holy Grail' type of situation, epitomized by such books as *King Solomon's Mines* by H. Rider Haggard or the movie *Raiders of the Lost Ark*. Send your hero out to recover something of awesome value which is being held by ruthless criminals, and you have an adventure story filled with suspense. These books are the purest examples of the form. The basic principle can be manipulated until it is suitable for any of the fiction genres, for there are as many impossible goals as there are people willing to strive for them.

From Rags to Riches

Suspense of a different kind is generated here. Now readers are eagerly anticipating the poor heroine's rise from abject poverty to a decent life.

With this theme you will immediately think of Catherine Cookson. In many of her books the situations described are so harrowing, and sympathy for the poor character so strong (remember the short chapter on heroes), that readers are practically urging her to *overcome*; to rise up and triumph over the cruel people who are keeping her down in the gutter by ruthlessly abusing and using her for their own benefit.

Once again linked sub-plots abound, and readers often follow the story through generations.

From Riches to Rags

Enter Danielle Steel and Barbara Taylor Bradford territory. The suspense in these novels is milked from a vast number of situations, but gains its intensity because of readers empathizing with a single, outstanding character looking back over an incident-packed life, or with several characters over succeeding generations of a dynasty.

There will always be a strong main plot, but because the families in these books are always large – and larger than life – the opportunities for a web of linked sub-plots are virtually endless.

Suspense also comes from waiting for the inevitable crash, the loss of fame and fortune, the realization that the simple things in life have value.

Reluctant Hero

Nobody does this better than Dick Francis. Although his heroes are usually involved with horse-racing, the theme can be used in any environment. The suspense comes from seeing an essentially ordinary, everyday bloke involved in activities totally outside and far above his experience. The opening lines of *Straight*, which I have quoted more than once, are a perfect example of how this ordinary person can be thrown in at the deep end.

Sometimes the hero is already successful, and quite rich, but always the suspense comes from watching someone moving into an unfamiliar and incredibly dangerous field and triumphing over the acknowledged experts (villains).

There are many other themes or situations that appear under a variety of labels, and often the distinctions are blurred. 'Beauty and the Beast' and 'The Triumph of Good Over Evil' are two, but those can be used to describe all or part of the novels I referred to respectively as typical of Danielle Steel or Catherine Cookson.

You will also notice that I said 'all or part of'. Although the basic theme of your novel might be the reluctant hero, under that umbrella there will be many incidents and situations, and each of those might be recognizable as being based on another stereotypical theme.

But you will also have realized very quickly that the labels I have given and a host more that you come up with are all taken straight from real life, albeit somewhat enlarged and exaggerated.

Just as the fears I mentioned in an earlier chapter are recognizable because they are common fears – a child starting school; an old person entering a home; people living in poverty frightened that there is not enough money in the purse; a rich man with the fear of not appearing to be free enough with his money – so the themes and situations that create spontaneous suspense are all around you, waiting to be used.

How to Confuse and Misinform to Create the Suspense of Uncertainty

Detective stories are littered with red herrings, and that's one of the classical methods used by authors to confuse. Defined in the dictionary as misleading clues, they obviously fit well into that particular genre. A bloodstained knife is found at the scene of the murder, the fingerprints on it belong to the security guard, he is the guilty man – but of course, he isn't.

However, what I did there was misinform you just a little to demonstrate a point. The whole of the definition of red herring includes the words, 'or distraction', so now what we have is a technique that can be taken out of detective fiction and used across genres.

Confuse, misinform, distract (always through your characters), and you will create suspense. All the way through your book, whether it be a puzzle or a rags-to-riches family saga, readers are trying to guess the outcome. If they succeed in their aim, you haven't necessarily lost them; they may still read on to see if they are right (though they are more likely to go straight to the last page), in order to bask in their astuteness.

But if you can keep them guessing to the end, they will be miffed, but pleased, too, that you have done a good job by maintaining the suspense to the very end. And there are as many ways of putting them off the track as there are stars in a cloudless night sky.

If you take an ordinary novel written in the single third person viewpoint, everything that goes on must be seen through your main character. However, although your main character will frequently be confused and misinformed, he can also do his own misinforming in order to confuse others. In the first instance, the readers will not realize what is happening. In the second they will, because they are privy to the leading character's thoughts, and know what he's up to.

Let's look at some methods by which our leading characters can be confused. We are many times told that we must never assume something to be correct. So, of course, you will make sure that your very human leading characters assume, and are wrong. They will assume that someone is telling them the truth. They will assume that their logical analysis of a situation points to an inevitable outcome, when we all know that few things follow the course of logic.

Assumptions and logical analysis taken together will prove doubly disastrous (if that's possible). If your hero is told that the villain is taking the Orient Express to Istanbul (the information is assumed to be correct), it is quite easy to find out the day and time of his arrival (logical analysis) and be there to intercept. Unfortunately, if the first bit of information was *misinformation*, racing ahead of the train to intercept it will be a waste of time.

No matter what genre your main characters operate in, they will always be watching and listening, drawing conclusions, acting on information. Some of their conclusions will be right, some wrong; they will be acting on information that is either true, or false.

If you mix and match, making your main characters subject to human fallibility and so correct only part of the time, you will have sown the seeds of uncertainty. And in the same way that unpredictable character reactions create suspense because readers are never sure what a character will do next, uncertainty will create suspense because your readers can never be certain of the outcome of any situation until it actually happens.

Confusion caused by your leading character misinforming others creates suspense in a different way. Let's suppose that your hero leaks false information to the villains, leading them to believe that *he* is taking the Orient Express to Istanbul. Readers' suspense now derives from wondering if the villains will fall for the ruse, and head off on a wild-goose chase.

Uncertainty can also be planted in your readers' minds simply by allowing your main character to indulge in some introspection during which several possible ways the story can develop are analysed.

Intelligent readers' thoughts will already have outstripped the action as they race ahead to examine possible consequences of main character/villain's reactions, and those readers will be feeling somewhat jittery as a result.

Although nothing actually happens during your deliberately suggestive period of introspection, by following certain hypothetical plot twists and reaching the inevitable disastrous conclusions you can perhaps offer certain outcomes that may not have occurred to readers. Because you, the writer, have planted it in their minds (through your character's introspection), it will be all the more believable, and so much more likely to build suspense.

Suspense Through the Use of Kipling's 'Honest Serving-men'

I keep six honest serving-men
(They taught me all I knew);

Their names are What and Why and When
And How and Where and Who.

Those lines were written by Rudyard Kipling in *Just So Stories*, in 'How the Camel got his Hump', and those six serving-men are often used by journalists to ensure that they have included every vital bit of information in an article.

But they are also an excellent guide for the author seeking to create suspense for, as I mentioned in Chapter Five, you must continually plant questions in readers' minds – and preferably make them appear insoluble. The easiest way of examining the usefulness of these serving-men is to list some well-known uses.

The 'whodunnit' is the detective novel in which the objective of both hero and reader is to identify the villain.

The 'whydunnit' asks not who committed a crime, but why it was committed.

The 'howdunnit' might refer to the famous 'locked room' detective mysteries. A body is discovered in a room, nobody else is present, death could not have been from suicide, and the door is locked from the inside. *The Murders in the Rue Morgue*, by Edgar Allan Poe, is probably the first and certainly the most famous example.

The serving-man called What is most easily recognizable in the science fiction, supernatural or horror novel, where something is happening that cannot be explained.

Our Mister Where is, of course, that back-bone of the novel involving a search for a fabulous lost treasure, while although Mister When is not quite so easy to pin down as the theme of one complete novel (other than time travel, when the answer usually comes fairly quickly), it is quite easy to see how the question might be asked many times during the course of a single book.

Apart from Mister When, these are all examples of the use of

Kipling's serving-men to arrive at a suspenseful theme for a book. But it is very easy to see that they will have their uses, across genres, as both the main theme for a novel or as questions to be asked from time to time. The examples given have been obvious and simplistic ways in which the six questions can and have been used. But by digging deeper, or using some of that famous lateral thinking, or brainstorming, it quickly becomes clear that there are many possibilities in each little word.

Take 'where', for example. For me this is one of the most intriguing of the six questions, because so many (if not all) novels are concerned with the main character's search for some-thing. Human beings will search for happiness, for romance, for wealth, for health, for fame, for self-fulfilment, for a lost relative, for vengeance, for justice, for a scientific breakthrough – and there must be many more. In books based on any of those themes, the question that provides the basis for suspense is 'where'?

But even though each of the six questions has a use as the theme for a complete book, that is not their main value as a tool for creating suspense. As themes, they will become lost, drowned in a sea of words. As questions to be asked time and time again they have the ability to disturb, to frighten, to sadden – indeed, to create any emotion you choose – but because they are questions, above all they demand an answer. And because, in a well-written book, that answer is rarely given until some time has passed, the result is suspense.

Creating Suspense Using Threats – Specific and Implied

Threats of any kind are frightening, and because they are concerned with something that is going to happen at some time in the future, they always create a degree of suspense.

Specific Threats

One kind of specific threat comes when a villain says, 'I'm going to kill you, Shapiro!' From that moment on, readers are looking over their shoulder for the hit-man with the rifle, the thug stepping out of the alley, the sharp knife pushed through the back of the seat at the theatre.

Another comes when a mother says to little Andrew, 'You'll get no pudding unless you eat all your dinner.'

In between those two extremes you might have the young woman saying, 'Simon, unless you give up gambling, our engagement is off,' which is neither the threat of cold-blooded murder nor a threat likely to cause a child to cry, but is certainly something that will have readers waiting, in suspense, to see which way the pendulum will swing.

Once again, what you are doing is making your readers wait, and wonder. In this kind of specific threat, there is a no-nonsense statement telling readers exactly what is going to happen, *unless . . .*

Unless what?

Well, in the case of Andrew, unless he eats all his dinner.

In Simon's case, unless he gives up gambling.

But there is another kind of specific threat which is also a no-nonsense statement telling readers exactly what is going to happen, because . . .

Usually, the reason will be revenge, retribution.

'I'm going to kill you *because I served twenty years in prison for a crime you committed.*'

'I'm going to kill you *because you stole my wife, my children, and my career.*'

'I'm going to break you, Carruthers, *because you reported my insider trading to the authorities and ruined my chances of a knighthood.*'

'I'm leaving you, Simon, *because you didn't give up gambling after all.*'

Implied Threats

Implied threats can be human, inanimate, or abstract. They can be against others, or against self (if against self, the threat becomes risk).

They are, as the name suggests, much more subtle, and we have already seen what might be mistaken for an implied threat in our study of character's actions in the chapter on foreshadowing.

But where foreshadowing is a technique that sets out to suggest what might happen in the future while at the same time trying to *hide* this intent, the implied threat is never a secret, and is often immediate.

For example, if the tough private eye is confronting a crooked casino owner in his office, and from the small window overlooking the roulette tables he sees the man's sadistic bodyguard wandering slowly across the room towards the stairs, this is not foreshadowing but an immediate, implied threat.

In the same way, if a man and woman are naked in the woman's bedroom and they hear the key in the front door that tells them her husband has arrived home from work early, there is the implied threat of discovery. The threat is immediate, the suspense is real.

In both cases, the threat may come to nothing. The bodyguard may see an acquaintance, and head for the bar. The woman's husband may have got the afternoon off work and come home early simply to pick up his golf clubs.

But now, as a direct result of nothing happening, those implied threats have created a definite change in the novel's atmosphere. In future, in similar situations, the implied threat will be there without any further effort on the part of the author.

Each time the man and woman retire to the bedroom, the readers will be listening for the key in the lock; whenever the detective returns to the casino's office – or to any other part of the casino – readers will be expecting the bodyguard to appear.

Through implied threats, you have created immediate suspense which will intensify each time the private eye or the two clandestine lovers get away with it.

Both of the above examples featured implied threats posed by humans. An example of an inanimate implied threat is the approach of a helicopter – or the sound of thunder, the crack of a gun – when climbers are making their way across a glacier beneath towering, snow-laden slopes (threat of avalanche). Or the same climbers crossing a fragile rope suspension bridge in torrential rain, and a rope snapping when they are halfway across (threat of a fatal plunge into the ravine).

All but one of the above examples are extremes taken from thriller or adventure situations. But as the illicit love scene shows, simply by shifting the location and changing the threat you can make the technique fit into your chosen genre.

In just the same way, this example of threat to self (or risk) can be manipulated to cross genres.

Some readers may have seen the film *The Wages of Fear*, which, if my memory is correct, was showing in the 1950s and starred the French actor Yves Montand. At the climax of the film, the star is driving a heavy truck containing nitroglycerine along winding roads with a steep drop on one side. He is laughing and singing, and in his exuberance he begins to swing the steering-wheel so that the truck begins to veer from one side of the road to the other.

The implied threat is there: if he continues to swing the heavy vehicle backwards and forwards across the road, he will drive over that steep drop. Inevitably, that is exactly what happens. If it had been halfway through the film, he would have survived. But this was the end. . . .

This is a threat against self in a high-risk situation; the character in the truck is risking his life.

But that same implied threat to self could just as easily feature a man going to the race-track with his week's wages in his pocket.

In Practice

Several times during the previous chapters I have suggested that a careful examination of your own or other people's lives will reveal much that will be of help when you come to work on the techniques being discussed in this book, and doing that now will again pay dividends by giving you a host of serviceable incidents or situations.

Spontaneous suspense is all around us, in the meaner streets we walk (dark, littered, filled with unexplained sounds or sinister figures); in the roads we travel (fog on motorways bringing visions of traffic accidents, lonely stretches in the Cairngorms warning of the consequences of a breakdown; halts at city-centre traffic lights with the the threat of car-jacking).

Uncertainty and confusion are caused when you are fed lies and misinformation. Even something as relatively trivial as your young son or daughter telling you, with wide-eyed innocence, that they will be home at six o'clock, can cause aching suspense when they have still not arrived by seven. Examination of your feelings, and the way that sequences of events can be adapted to create an adult situation in fiction, will reveal many possibilities.

Kipling's famous questions are always with us. Who are you going out with tonight? What time will you be home? I know you didn't work late at the office – so where were you? As you see how those questions can have unexpected and often harmful ramifications in real life, so you will understand how their use in fiction can help you to build suspense.

Implied and specific threats can be demonstrated in just the one real-life example. If you have ever known anybody who has been in trouble with paying their mortgage – and, goodness, that problem is all too common – then you will understand the different effects of implied (failure to clear arrears may result in further action) and specific (the building society is about to repossess your house).

12 Using Hooks, Cliffhangers and Time-limits

After dealing doggedly with such terms as foreshadowing, linked sub-plots and the third person impersonal, you will probably find it something of a relief to be confronted by the simple words at the head of this chapter.

They are almost self-explanatory, but behind their straightforward sounds there lies a power that has been used by storytellers since the days when wandering minstrels strolled from village to village spinning their colourful yarns.

You reach out to grab hold of your readers. When you've got them, you make sure they don't go away. That takes care of the workings of the first two terms, and although the function of the third isn't quite so clear, the way its use can create tremendous suspense will shortly be revealed.

In this chapter you will learn how to:

- Open chapters with hooks
- Close chapters with cliffhangers
- Use specific time-limits to create riveting suspense
- Use undefined time-limits to create maximum suspense

Open Chapters with Hooks

The most famous hook of all is, 'Meanwhile, back at the ranch.' (It's also a transition – a move in time and place – but that's by the by.)

But, Westerns apart, I could start and finish this section within three lines. All I need say is, look again at that now-familiar quotation from *Straight*.

In his opening paragraph to that book, Dick Francis is almost guilty of going over the top. He has mentioned someone's life, their business, their gadgets, their horses, their mistress, and implies that – for the book's suddenly put-upon hero – stirring them together creates an explosive, life-threatening mixture. It's almost as if the whole story has been précised in one fell swoop, and although for Dick Francis it is an aproach that proves stunningly effective, I would advise writers to draft their hooks with a little more restraint.

Those little headings that we discussed in the chapter on fore-shadowing are also excellent examples of hooks (an illustration of the way fiction techniques have more than one function).

Chapter Twenty of *King Solomon's Mines* by H. Rider Haggard has the heading 'We Abandon Hope', and is followed by the neat, old-fashioned hook:

I can give no adequate description of the horrors of the night which follows.

Those are both carefully crafted devices to ensure that the reader keeps reading, and although the sentence is just the first of a long paragraph, it is representative of the whole.

This next, more modern example of a hook, is the opening line of the first chapter of *If Tomorrow Comes*, by Sidney Sheldon:

She undressed slowly, dreamily, and when she was naked, she selected a bright red negligee to wear so that the blood would not show.

© Sidney Sheldon 1985. Extract from *If Tomorrow Comes* by Sidney Sheldon. Reproduced by permission of HarperCollins Publishers Ltd.

Again, this is only a part of the opening paragraph, but as with the quotation from H. Rider Haggard it is the most instantly arresting portion and has been placed at the beginning to draw the reader into the story.

Finally, another example of Stephen King's work, this time the first line of the prologue to *Insomnia*.

No one – least of all Dr. Litchfield – came right out and told Ralph Roberts that his wife was going to die, but there came a time when Ralph understood without needing to be told.

© Stephen King 1994. Extract from *Insomnia* by Stephen King. Reproduced by permission of Hodder and Stoughton Ltd.

More follows, in the same vein, but once again the job has been done in the first line, or few lines. The hook has been cast, and almost assuredly swallowed.

But giving examples of hooks is of little use unless students – who are here to learn how to write their own – carefully study them to see exactly why they are effective. And the one glaring quality they have is the art of leaving something unsaid.

It's as if the author is saying, 'I bet you can't guess what I'm talking about!'

The old-fashioned writer of thrillers or adventure novels would come right out and declare that something horrible was about to happen, frequently doing it that way because the story was written from the first-person viewpoint. A famous example is *The Thirty-nine Steps*, by John Buchan, in which the hero, Richard Hannay begins one chapter by saying:

I sat down on the very crest of the path and took stock of my position.

a wonderfully innocuous hook which invites readers to recapitulate with him.

As time passed, authors became more subtle (though not necessarily better writers) and readers expected to see more veiled threats, insinuations or suggestions. Sidney Sheldon plants in your imagination a red negligee soaked in blood but tells you no more; Stephen King tells you a woman is going to die – surely the most shocking of hooks – but gives no details and forces you to read on.

It is very easy to see how that first example, by Sidney Sheldon, might be manipulated so that it becomes a hook suitable for almost any genre:

> She dressed slowly, and with care, selecting as her outer garment the coat she had worn to Phil's funeral. When she closed the door behind her, she knew it was for the last time.

Yes, it could mean anything, or nothing – and that, probably, is the clearest definition of the very best of hooks, and what you should aim for when writing them.

Close Chapters with Cliffhangers

The most blatant of all cliffhangers is the chapter ending that has a dying man gurgling, 'It was . . . it was . . .', and expiring before he utters the name of his killer.

The modern writer who always devised the most infuriating cliffhangers was the late Adam Hall (Elleston Trevor). He enjoyed nothing more than leaving the reader in the highest possible suspense as something terrible is about to happen at the end of a chapter, then starting the next chapter on a completely different tack with apparently no intention of revealing what had happened.

When he did provide the answer, it would frequently be in an almost casual aside.

The *Scorpion Signal* by this outstanding thriller writer provides many examples. At the end of Chapter Four, after a tremendous build-up, Agent Quiller is sitting in a stationary car at night, with his field director, Bracken, as the searching Russian militia close in for the kill.

> I got comfortable in my seat and moved the stick into low and kept my foot down on the clutch and put my fingers against the starter key and watched the light flood brightly across the buildings as I waited to know if the trap we were sitting in was going to spring shut.

The end of a paragraph, the end of a chapter, written as two long sentences (the above is the second) to increase the suspense, with no punctuation other than the separating full stop.

A wonderful cliffhanger.

But at the start of the next chapter, the readers are taken somewhere else.

> 'Good evening, little mother.'
> Her head came up sharply. She was sitting with her back to the wall of the hallway, her cracked, black shoes resting on the edge of the slow-combustion stove, the naked bulb throwing light on her white hair.

© Trevor Enterprises Inc., 1979. (See page 128 for details.)

All very atmospheric. But this is Quiller talking, in a different part of the city. So, what happened? Did the trap snap shut? It is as if the cliffhanger is being extended. There are now two things left unexplained: what happened at the end of the previous chapter, and where Quiller is now, and for some time readers are never quite sure if that first question is ever to be answered.

The second question is answered first. Then, in just the kind of casual aside I talked about, tucked away in the middle of a long paragraph, we learn from Quiller's thoughts that:

> The second militia patrol had gone hounding straight past us and I'd used the back streets towards the ring road, working my way out of the search area . . .

© Trevor Enterprises Inc., 1979. Extracts from *The Scorpion Signal* by Adam Hall. Reproduced by permission of A.M. Heath & Co. Ltd on behalf of the author.

In this case, as in many others, the author has written an outstanding action sequence filled with high tension, and closed the chapter just as the scene reached its climax. The cliffhanger was superb, the description of the outcome something of an anti-climax; it's quite possible that was a deliberate literary device to create frustration in the reader so that the next action sequence becomes all the more welcome, and again we have an interesting subject for debate.

Raymond Chandler is most often quoted for the wonderfully laconic wisecracks scattered so effortlessly by his private detective, Philip Marlowe. But all Chandler's novels are exciting thrillers, and contain their share of cliffhangers.

At the end of Chapter Six of *The Big Sleep*, Marlowe is breaking into a house:

> I kicked the French window in, used my hat for a glove and pulled out most of the lower small pane of glass. I could now reach in and draw a bolt that fastened the window to the sill. The rest was easy. There was no top bolt. The catch gave. I climbed in and pulled the drapes off my face.
>
> Neither of the two people in the room paid any attention to the way I came in, although only one of them was dead.

© Raymond Chandler 1939. Extract from *The Big Sleep* (Penguin Books, 1948). Reproduced by permission of Penguin Books Ltd.

Like Adam Hall, Raymond Chandler proceeds some way into the next chapter before letting the reader into his secret – in this case, one long descriptive paragraph before revealing the identity of the living person, another three before turning to the dead man. But because there is no change of scene there is not the same sense of dislocation; readers wait with patience rather than frustration, because they know the answer will come.

A more typical example of a cliffhanger comes at the end of Chapter Fourteen of the same novel:

'Oh, hell,' he said. 'You win.' He stood up and slipped the Colt into his side pocket. His left hand went up inside his coat. He was holding it there, his face twisted with disgust, when the door buzzer rang and kept on ringing.

© Raymond Chandler 1939. Extract from *The Big Sleep* (Penguin Books, 1948). Reproduced by permission of Penguin Books Ltd.

The reaction following this one is much more immediate, yet still the author dangles the reader.

In the first three, short paragraphs of the next chapter he gives the varying reactions of the three people shocked by the sudden sound of the buzzer. A gun is taken out of a drawer. There is an exchange of words, and now we are six paragraphs into the next chapter and in the seventh the buzzer is replaced by an impatient rapping at the door and, finally, the door is opened.

There is a pattern emerging here, isn't there?

Although different authors handle the technique in very individual ways, and even the same authors vary it to suit the situation – or simply to ring the changes – it is becoming clear that, after a cliffhanger, the suspense can be and usually is maintained by delaying disclosure of the outcome.

Adam Hall often takes the technique to extremes by moving right away from the scene and seemingly forgetting that a cliffhanger existed. In one example, Raymond Chandler handles the disclosure in a leisurely fashion – because the nature of the cliffhanger permitted it (one dead person, another comatose) – while in another he does it more frenetically, with violent reactions, short, bitter arguments, and while all this is going on the cliffhanger (insistent buzzing at the door) is intensifying the suspense.

Perhaps the supreme example of squeezing every ounce of suspense out of a cliffhanger comes from *Misery*, by Stephen King, a novel in which Paul Sheldon is kept prisoner by the insane Annie Wilkes. Paul has two broken legs, and spends most of the book lying in bed.

Chapter Twenty closes with the prick of a needle in Paul Sheldon's arm. When Chapter Twenty-one opens he knows what the prick was, because suddenly he cannot lift his arms from the bed. But he doesn't know why Annie has given him the shot. A complete chapter goes by, with one casual bit of foreshadowing (he hears a wooden thunk, a metallic clunk), but still nothing is revealed. At the end of this chapter, the wooden thump is heard again.

There are now two cliffhangers spread over two chapters (the prick of a needle; a wooden thunk), the first still not explained but carried forward to join the second in creating screaming suspense that comes to a climax in the third chapter – but for the sake of those fans of Stephen King who have not yet read the book, that's all I'm going to reveal.

Use Specific Time-limits to Create Riveting Suspense

The vital ingredients needed to create suspense by using a specific time-limit are a clear definition of the time-limit, some time-consuming obstacles, and constant reminders of how time is running short.

I quoted a visit to the dentist when talking about viewpoint, in the section on 'The "do know" principle' (in Chapter Nine). The point I was making was that it can be very frightening when you don't know what is going to happen, but positively terrifying when you know something gruesome is going to happen, and know exactly what it is.

The use of a specific time limit is the logical extension of that principle. It can be used in both cases, the 'do know' and the 'don't know', and is probably the most frequently employed and true to life of all the literary techniques for creating suspense.

In real life:

Your dental appointment is for 3.15. You must sit in the waiting-room, trembling, until your name is called.

The interview before a panel for the vacant executive position is at 9.00 a.m. Anticipating it ruins a night's sleep and your breakfast.

The deadline for entries in an important short-story competition is three days away, and you have no idea what to write.

In fiction:

The millionaire is told by the man who kidnapped his daughter that if the ransom is not handed over by dawn, she will die – and he cannot raise the money.

The assistant office manager who has made disastrous decisions knows the boss will be back from holiday in exactly seven days time, and the only man who can save the situation – the other businessman – is out of the country.

The hero racing through the night in his Aston Martin

knows that the express will scream through at midnight – but it's already 11.30, he has thirty miles to go and the engine is misfiring.

Establishing a specific time limit is a simple device to create tension, and it is highly effective because it is a problem we have all faced: almost every situation in modern life is governed by the clock.

Television programmes such as *Ready, Steady, Cook* (for those who don't know, it has two cooks preparing a meal against the clock) employ the time-limit principle, and make it effective by having the presenter call out the time remaining at frequent intervals.

When writing fiction, the same method is used. You remind your readers how time is passing, but you do it in the most natural way. Each time the hero in the Aston Martin comes up against an obstacle – a flooded road, level-crossing gates closed, traffic lights on red – he looks at his watch and sees that time is running out. The millionaire will consult his watch, but he will also have the police reminding him that there are only so many hours left.

Use Undefined Time-limits to Create Maximum Suspense

The vital ingredients needed to create suspense using an undefined time-limit are a clear explanation of the nature of the time-limit, some time-consuming obstacles, and one or more false alarms.

If, in real life, the suspense of waiting for a known zero hour turns you into a quivering jelly, what will be the effect of waiting for an unknown zero hour; how will you cope if you have been told to turn up at the surgery, and wait until the dentist can fit you in?

Each time the intercom clicks, you could be called. Each time the call is for somebody else, some more of your meagre store of courage will leak away.

Perhaps because many of Stephen King's horror stories rely on recognizable situations to create fear, the finest example of the technique of using undefined time-limits that I know of comes from one of his novels. Once again it is *Misery*, and of course it is the imprisoned Paul Sheldon who is sweating it out.

Paul's situation reaches the stage when he is able to sit in a wheel-chair. Crazy Annie Wilkes wants him to write a novel specially for her, but she has provided the wrong typing-paper. In an insane rage, she goes to town to get the correct paper, leaving Paul locked in the room, in his wheel-chair, without pain-killers.

Paul picks the lock, opens the door, and manages to manoeuvre the wheel-chair out through the narrow opening. And now this is an extremely frightening situation: a crippled man in constant agony, trapped in a wheel-chair, has broken out of his room to find medication. He knows Annie Wilkes will kill him (or worse) if she returns before he gets back into his room – but he doesn't know how long it will be before Annie does return.

This time the suspense cannot be intensified simply by having the hero look at his watch. Time in that sense means nothing, because the time-limit is undefined.

What Stephen King does instead is to make Paul's every movement incredibly difficult and painful, thus slowing him down. In addition there are natural obstacles. He has to pick up a bobby-pin to pick the lock, and cannot reach the floor from his wheel-chair. When he does succeed in picking the pin up, he then drops it. He cannot find the medication; when he does, he hears a car and must wait in an agony of suspense until it . . . drives past. He decides to visit Annie's sitting-room, and knocks an ornament off a table. He tries the telephone, and discovers the cord has been ripped from the socket. And when, finally, he hears a second car and this time it is Annie and she turns into the drive, he is still in her sitting-room – and the wheel-chair jams in the doorway of his room when he is desperately trying to get in and re-lock the door.

Throughout this long scene the readers know Annie Wilkes will return sooner or later. Because they are already hooked by Paul's predicament, and living it with him, every delay affecting him and driving him deeper into terror does exactly the same for them. And when he hears that second car approaching, and knows, *knows*, that it is Annie returning and he is still a long way from his room, the terror for Paul and the readers becomes unbearable.

Although the writing is superb, this is suspense of a basic and very dramatic kind. There is little subtlety. Emotions are raw and exposed, as indeed they are with all time-limit situations. But those situations are ones with which every reader can all too easily identify – and quote their own horror stories – and, for writers of all abilities, they are marvellously effective ways of creating almost instant suspense.

In Practice

All four of the techniques described in this chapter are indispensable tools in the writer's efforts to create suspense.

If I were to choose two from the four as being of greater importance, then I would pick hooks and cliffhangers, and for these reasons: almost every book has chapters with beginnings and endings, and it is at those natural pauses that you must work hard to prevent your readers from making the pause permanent.

I spoke earlier about breaks (scene and chapter) being inserted at the point where the opportunity for creating suspense was at its highest. Hooks and cliffhangers can also be used between scenes, and quite often, when you read through an unbroken chapter, you will see a place where you have written an obvious cliffhanger and let it slip by unnoticed. In such cases, do some minor rewriting. Draw attention to the cliffhanger by inserting a simple space break immediately after it, and notice what an intensifying effect a couple of blank lines can have on the suspense within that chapter.

I think enough has been said about time-limits. In this time-mad world, all you need do is look at life and you will see the effects of specific and undefined time-limits. I have used a visit to the dentist as an illustration, but throughout your day you will find other examples – involving you, or other people – that can be adapted for use in fiction.

If you write the Joanna Trollope type of book in which quite ordinary middle-class families struggle through life and loves, many everyday examples of time limits can be lifted and used without change, and will at once strike a chord with your readers. If you write other kinds of book – mystery, adventure, thrillers or horror – it is better if you ask that perennial question, 'what if?', for as many times as it takes to reach the dizzy heights of suspense necessary to suit your story.

To see what that does to suspense, try asking 'what if?' in relation to our patient waiting to see the dentist. You will be amazed at what you come up with!

Conclusion

As you have progressed through this book I am quite sure that one important point has become more and more obvious. It is that every technique discussed and dissected and extolled repeatedly as being ideal for creating suspense, has one or more other uses.

This is probably true of all the thousand-and-one techniques used by fiction writers to create a story that will firstly, and most importantly, persuade lovers of fiction to read that story from beginning to end but will also, in the long run, create one that lingers in the minds of their readers.

But without undervaluing those other uses, or denying their indispensability, let's now forget them.

My sole purpose has been to help you achieve that first aim of persuading readers to start your book at the beginning and put it down at 'The End', and if, along the way, you also create a memorable work of fiction, then what that proves is that creating suspense in fiction produces more than one result.

We have discovered a welcome by-product when setting out to achieve a different aim.

Creating Suspense in Fiction has been about anticipation. Looking back, I see now that this is the first time I've used that word, and what it means – according to one dictionary definition – is 'looking forward'.

When reading fiction, people look forward, and when they look forward they experience a variety of emotions. But whether they look forward with joy or fear, with hope or despair, with love or with grief, they are anticipating. The writer has, in one way or another, let them know that something – good or bad – is going to happen; by some mysterious means, they have been put in suspense. What this book has done – if I have succeeded – is to take the mystery out of the process by showing you some of the means.

You know now that the suspense in the sudden, heavy silence of a dense pine forest can be used to instil fear in readers as you take your government agent out of his car and he realizes, when stepping across the ditch, that the birds have stopped singing.

You know that the intense fear that causes your hands to tremble and your mouth to go dry when waiting for a dental appointment can be the fear of the unknown, or of the known, and that by putting your characters in that same position – intensified a thousand times because the time and the place have been created by you for atmosphere, and at the end of a known or unknown time what awaits them is a thousand times more deadly – you will create unbearable suspense.

And you know, too, from your own observation and close analysis of the methods described in this book, that just as suspense is an abstract emotion that people experience in their minds, so you, the writer, cannot create that abstract emotion without the help of your characters.

I think that is an excellent point at which to close.

Further Reading

Grant-Adamson, Lesley, *Teach Yourself Writing Crime Fiction* (Hodder & Stoughton, 1996)

Joseph, Richard, *Bestsellers* (Summersdale Publishers, 1997)

Jute, André, *Writing a Thriller* (A & C Black, 1986)

Legat, Michael, *An Author's Guide to Publishing*, 3rd edn (Robert Hale, 1998)

—— *Plotting the Novel* (Robert Hale, 1992)

—— *Understanding Publishers' Contracts* (Robert Hale, 1992)

Clark, Tom; Brohaugh, William; Woods, Bruce; Strickland, Bill; Blocksom, Peter (Eds) *Handbook of Novel Writing* (F & W Publications, Cincinnati, 1992)

Taylor Pianka, Phyllis, *How to Write Romances* (F & W Publications, Cincinnati, 1998)

Useful Addresses

The Society of Authors
84 Drayton Gardens
London SW10 9SB
Tel: 020 7373 6642

The Writers' and Artists' Yearbook
A & C Black
35 Bedford Row
London WC1R 4JH
Tel: 020 7242 0946

The Writer's Handbook
Macmillan Ltd
25 Ecclestone Place
London SW1V 9NF
Tel: 020 7881 8000

Writers News
P.O. Box 4
Nairn
Scotland IV12 4HU
Tel: 01667 454 441

Web Sites

Encyclopaedia Britannica
http://www.eb.com

Jacqui Bennett Writers Bureau
http://www.jacquibwb.ndirect.co.uk

Literature Live Network (Arts Council of England)
http://www.liveliterature.net

The Magik House
http://www.magikhouse.com

Webster's Dictionary (WWWebster's)
http://www.m-w.com/netdict.htm

Index